The convenience cook

125 Best Recipes for Easy Homemade Meals Using Time-Saving Foods from Boxes, Bottles, Cans & More

Judith Finlayson

D1307307

Robert
ROSE

The Convenience Cook
Text copyright © 2003 Judith Finlayson
Photographs copyright © 2003 Robert Rose Inc.

All rights reserved. The use of any part of this publication reproduced, transmitted in any form or by any means, electronic, mechanical, recording or otherwise, or stored in a retrieval system, without the prior consent of the publisher is an infringement of the copyright law. In the case of photocopying or other reprographic copying of the material, a licence must be obtained from the Canadian Reprography Collective before proceeding.

For complete cataloguing information, see page 186.

Disclaimer
The recipes in this book have been carefully tested by our kitchen and our tasters. To the best of our knowledge, they are safe and nutritious for ordinary use and users. For those people with food or other allergies, or who have special food requirements or health issues, please read the suggested contents of each recipe carefully and determine whether or not they may create a problem for you. All recipes are used at the risk of the consumer.

We cannot be responsible for any hazards, loss or damage that may occur as a result of any recipe use.

For those with special needs, allergies, requirements or health problems, in the event of any doubt, please contact your medical adviser prior to the use of any recipe.

Design & Production: PageWave Graphics Inc.
Editor: Carol Sherman
Copy Editor: Julia Armstrong
Recipe Tester: Jennifer MacKenzie
Photography: Mark T. Shapiro
Food Stylist: Kate Bush
Props Stylist: Charlene Erricson
Colour Scans: Colour Technologies

Cover Image: Chicken Curry (see recipe, page 109)
Photo page 4: Chinese Pepper Steak (see recipe, page 128)

The publisher and author wish to express their appreciation to the following suppliers of props used in the food photography:

DISHES, LINENS AND ACCESSORIES

Homefront
371 Eglinton Ave. W.
Toronto, Ontario, M5N 1A3
Tel: (416) 488-3189
www.homefrontshop.com

Caban
396 St. Clair Ave. W.
Toronto, Ontario, M5P 3N3
Tel: (416) 654-3316
www.caban.com

FLATWARE

Gourmet Settings Inc.
245 West Beaver Creek Rd., Unit 10
Richmond Hill, Ontario, L4B 1L1
Tel: 1-800-551-2649
www.gourmetsettings.com

We acknowledge the financial support of the Government of Canada through the Book Publishing Industry Development Program (BPIDP) for our publishing activities.

Published by Robert Rose Inc.
120 Eglinton Avenue East, Suite 800, Toronto, Canada M4P 1E2
Tel: (416) 322-6552   Fax: (416) 322-6936

Printed in Canada
1 2 3 4 5 6 7 FP 09 08 07 06 05 04 03

Acknowledgments

Once again, my deepest thanks to all those who have worked so hard to produce this beautiful book, our third as a creative team: Mark Shapiro, whose outstanding pictures keep getting better all the time, and the group at PageWave Graphics — Andrew Smith, Joseph Gisini, Kevin Cockburn and Daniella Zanchetta — who do such a great job of integrating all the visual elements with the text; food stylist Kate Bush, who makes all my recipes look perfectly delectable and props stylist Charlene Erricson, who so aptly sets the stage; Jennifer MacKenzie and Audrey King, recipe testers, par excellence, and the many friends and neighbors who tasted recipes in development and provided valuable feedback; and, of course, my eagle-eyed editor, Carol Sherman, who keeps me in line, on time and in remarkably good humor. Special thanks to my husband, Bob Dees, for his professional insight as well as his personal support and my dear daughter, Meredith, whose interest in food and budding culinary skills are a delight to behold.

641.555
F512c

JAN 1 4 2004
GERMANTOWN COMMUNITY LIBRARY
GERMANTOWN, WI 53022

GERMANTOWN COMMUNITY LIBRARY
GERMANTOWN, WI 53022

Contents

Introduction **6**

The Time-Efficient Pantry 9

Prepared Ingredients 10

Pantry Supplies 11

Fresh Basics 11

Basic Spices and Flavorings 12

The Shopping Plan 12

Appetizers, Snacks and Sandwiches **14**

Soups **36**

Salads **52**

Eggs and Meatless Mains **68**

Fish and Seafood **88**

Poultry **106**

Beef, Pork and Lamb **124**

Pasta and Pizza **146**

Desserts **164**

Index **187**

Introduction

GIVEN OUR TIME-PRESSED LIVES, most people are constantly looking for ways to prepare great-tasting and nutritious food in a hurry. We don't have time to shop every day and little or no interest in slaving over a hot stove. Worse still, by the end of the day we're often too exhausted to even think about the nitty-gritty of meal preparation. So it's not surprising we're vulnerable to eating on the run — grabbing fast food or ordering the same old takeout, even though the mere thought of how much salt and saturated fat such food contains induces indigestion, if not more serious concerns about clogged arteries and sky-rocketing blood pressure.

While we don't deliberately set out to make poor food choices, it's easy to be coerced into unhealthy eating patterns by the demands of daily living. For most people — unless we're among the lucky few with a personal chef — regularly consuming tastier and more nutritious food means making it ourselves. The problem is, preparing healthful and delicious food on a daily basis is no easy task. But thanks to the food industry help is at hand. Today's consumers can choose from a wide array of commercially prepared ingredients that can be used to create appetizing home-cooked meals while shortcutting preparation time. This includes a wide range of products, such as "fresh" refrigerated soups, a variety of sauces and stuffed pastas, already cooked meats and dehydrated foods, among others. The problem is, given this abundance of fully cooked and partially prepared foods, it's easy to forget that convenience-enhanced ingredients have a long tradition. In fact, for centuries people have been using manufactured food products to jump-start the cooking process or add a hit of flavor to simple foods.

"Convenience foods" such as sausages, mustards, vinegars and olive oil have been around so long that we take them for granted. Because we don't think of them as prepared foods, we're vulnerable to being seduced by the lure of packaged products that promise to deliver tasty meals in a flash. But deglazing the pan with a spoonful of Dijon mustard and a glass of white wine can do more for a fried pork chop than a bottle of the most expensive marinara sauce or a can of cream

---

CONVENIENCE COOKING

- ✦ is built around ingredients that come from jars, bottles, boxes, bags and cans
- ✦ uses ingredients that are likely to be on hand
- ✦ has a minimum number of easy-to-follow steps
- ✦ is usually on the table in less than 30 minutes
- ✦ tastes as good as made-from-scratch

of mushroom soup. And a mere splash of extra virgin olive oil enhanced with a squirt of fresh lemon juice and a few turns of the pepper mill are all it takes to transform a can of tuna into a delicious lunch. Add some finishing touches — capers, finely chopped pickled hot peppers and a sprinkle of thinly sliced green onion — and you have a genuine treat, one that was created by combining processed foods with a smattering of fresh ingredients.

The truth is, I consistently use a wide range of convenience foods as handy tools to help me speed up the preparation of tasty meals. I always have a few jars of good pasta sauce in the pantry and a wide selection of condiments on the refrigerator door, not to mention a package or two of smoked salmon and a bag of shelled and deveined shrimp in the freezer. In fact, there are many convenience foods I couldn't live without, including canned salmon and tuna. They are indispensable assistants to the management of my domestic life.

Take frozen and canned fruit and vegetables, for instance: in addition to their long shelf life, canned and frozen produce have value-added components that reduce kitchen prep time. The produce has been washed, peeled when necessary, and often sliced or cut. Moreover, studies show that when picked at their peak of ripeness and quickly processed, frozen and canned fruit and vegetables are likely to have as many nutrients as their "fresh" counterparts. For most of the year, fresh produce arrives in your kitchen after several days of travel, then sits in a store until purchased and, once again, in your refrigerator until it is used. There's an argument to be made that expertly processed frozen or canned produce is actually "fresher" than much of the fresh produce sold today. And if you're concerned that artificial additives and pesticides are synonymous with "processed," think again. As manufacturers recognize the growing market for "natural" foods, more and more processed foods and products, such as soups, sauces and juices, are certified organic.

MAXIMIZE CONVENIENCE

Look for the highlighted **Maximize Convenience** text throughout the book. It lists the ingredients in specific recipes that will produce the speediest results. And keep an eye out for the **Easy Extras** boxes, which suggest quick ways of adding flavor and/or variety to many recipes.

In my book, I emphasize that consistent good eating is a two-pronged approach: it requires a repertoire of fast and easy recipes and an organized approach to shopping built around foods that maximize convenience in a variety of ways. Because processed food often lacks flavor, achieving great made-from-scratch taste usually involves customization. By combining convenience products with your favorite ingredients and seasonings and adding a fresh ingredient or two as a finishing touch, you can create delicious dishes that usually take less than 30 minutes to prepare.

In recent years, proponents of "slow food" have drawn our attention to the beauty of fresh ingredients simply prepared — an approach to eating I respect and admire. Ideally I, too, would like to source squeaky-fresh asparagus, flavorful heirloom tomatoes, organic free range chickens and artisanal cheese and cook with these superb ingredients every day. But given the reality of my workaday life, this is simply not possible. While I aim to create the ideal as often as I can, most days I just want to cook delicious, nutritious food that my family will enjoy and I can prepare in a limited time frame. And over the years, I've come to recognize that doing this on a regular basis requires more than a few good "fast and easy" recipes.

While the recipes in this book will certainly enable you to produce great-tasting meals in a hurry, they can't single-handedly ensure that

THE CONVENIENCE EQUATION

EASE PLUS EXPEDIENCE = QUALITY

With easy-to-prepare recipes built around foods that maximize convenience, you can quickly prepare delicious meals with old-fashioned homemade flavor.

you will eat delicious food with old-fashioned homemade flavor every day. There's little point in having a favorite recipe that takes only 20 minutes to prepare if you need to stop at a grocery store on the way home to buy the ingredients. Suddenly, the start-to-finish time on that convenient recipe is likely to be an hour or more. For most people, making a commitment to cook regularly at home requires a minimum of organization. You'll need to ensure that your kitchen is well stocked with fresh ingredients that keep well, a good selection of frozen and canned food, and bottled and packaged ingredients with a long shelf life. Depending upon your lifestyle, you may need to develop a weekly meal plan and shop every seven days for the ingredients that will get you through the duration.

As the British food writer Nigel Slater says in his book *Appetite*, "Good eating is as much about shopping as cooking" — an approach with which I totally agree. Even if you're on a tight budget, I recommend buying a jar of Dijon mustard, a selection of good wine vinegars and the best extra virgin olive oil you can afford. These simple ingredients can be used to inject flavor and life into many foods. To suit his lifestyle, Nigel Slater always buys the best cheese, bread, olives and salami he can find. While a good antipasto platter can be an ideal appetizer or even a mealtime solution, it doesn't solve the problem of what to eat on Thursday if you bought the perfect baguette on Saturday and in the interim it has morphed into something resembling a stone.

I'm not suggesting you cook for convenience all the time. There are days when nothing is more appealing than spending hours in the kitchen making labor-intensive dishes for a special event or just because you feel like it. But remaining committed to cooking at home means that the makings of a meal should always be on hand so that you can arrive home any day of the week, locate the ingredients you need and prepare your chosen recipe within an acceptable time frame. You'll also want a few tricks up your sleeve that make entertaining a pleasure or inspire confidence in your ability to cope with unexpected guests.

THE TIME-EFFICIENT PANTRY

On any trip to the supermarket these days, it's impossible to avoid the bonanza of prepared foods designed to help us produce dinner in record-breaking time. Surrounded by bottled sauces, ready-to-bake pizza crusts, fresh stuffed pastas and cooked rotisserie chickens, it's easy to forget that nature has also provided us with some quintessential convenience foods. Consider a perfectly ripe avocado splashed with oil and vinegar, a thinly sliced cucumber tossed in a dressing made with rice vinegar, or a flawlessly poached egg. All take only minutes to prepare, and the basic ingredients will keep refrigerated or on the shelf for at least a week.

My point is that quick isn't necessarily synonymous with processed. And although processed foods are great time-savers, many come up short on taste. Simply stated, they usually benefit from the addition of fresh ingredients. It's amazing how much better bottled Alfredo sauce tastes with a bit of lemon zest and how just a sprinkling of finely chopped parsley adds color and zip to a bean salad straight out of the bottle. Even better, once you get the hang of combining prepared foods with an extra ingredient or two, you've opened the door to a host of possibilities. Consider, for instance, that old standby: bottled tomato sauce. In this book, it is the basis for such recipes as Spinach Tortellini Bake, Sausage Bolognese, Shrimp in Tomato Sauce with Feta, Simple Succotash, Chicken and Black Bean Chili and Italian-Style Chicken Cutlets, among others.

> **WATCH THE SALT**
> When using prepared foods, it is important to keep your eye on the salt, as they are usually very high in sodium. In addition, the quantities vary from brand to brand, which makes it difficult to know exactly how much salt to add to any recipe. The safest strategy is to use salt with extreme caution in any recipes that contain prepared ingredients. If it turns out that you underestimated the quantity you need, it's no problem to add salt just before serving.

Producing meals that taste homemade in a matter of minutes demands that essentials are always on hand. To ensure that your cupboard is appropriately stocked, I have listed the basic ingredients required to make the most of the recipes at the beginning of each chapter. These fall into three general categories: prepared ingredients, pantry supplies and fresh basics. In addition, you will need an assortment of dried spices.

PREPARED INGREDIENTS

These ingredients save you time and help you produce outstanding results with a minimum of effort because someone else has already done part or all of the prep work — chopping, mixing, shredding and even cooking. Although some of these ingredients are relatively recent additions to supermarket shelves, many — such as mustards, Asian sauces, canned soups, cooked legumes and prepared pastas (fresh, frozen and dried) — have been around for quite a while. This category includes:

+ frozen and canned foods, such as meat, fish, seafood, vegetables and fruit
+ prepared sauces
+ soups and stocks
+ mayonnaise, mustard, ketchup, chili sauce and other condiments
+ precooked deli foods, such as rotisserie chickens and roast beef
+ cake mix
+ prepared puddings, ice cream and sorbet
+ vinegars and oils
+ pasta and noodles (fresh, frozen and dried)
+ many other packaged ingredients too numerous to list

PERFORATED VEGETABLE BAGS

Perforated vegetable bags, which can be purchased in the section of the supermarket where plastic wrap is located, are an excellent investment in convenience and freshness. The tiny vents allow in moisture, adding storage time to vegetables and fruits. When you return home from shopping, transfer fresh produce to these bags, then store in the crisper drawer. The bags can be washed and reused several times, making them quite economical.

PANTRY SUPPLIES

There are some ingredients no kitchen should be without as they are required in many recipes. These include:

- ✦ basic sugars — confectioner's (icing), brown and granulated
- ✦ all-purpose flour
- ✦ rice, including long-grain white and Arborio
- ✦ butter
- ✦ cooking chocolate

BAGGED, WASHED SALAD GREENS

I can't say enough positive things about those bags of washed salad greens that now drape the produce departments in food stores. Not only are they a tremendous time-saver, but because they are packed in vented bags, which extend storage time, they allow you to have fresh, healthful greens every day of the week. Add chopped red or green onion, celery, cherry tomatoes – whatever you have on hand – and toss with your favorite dressing. Just make sure you buy brands that include an expiration date, and use them before their time is up.

FRESH BASICS

Fresh basics include ingredients that are quick to prepare and that can be stored in the refrigerator for a week or more. These include:

- ✦ eggs
- ✦ cucumbers
- ✦ avocados
- ✦ broccoli and cauliflower florets, washed and cut
- ✦ celery
- ✦ baby carrots, peeled and washed
- ✦ lemons
- ✦ grape and cherry tomatoes
- ✦ parsley
- ✦ green or red onions
- ✦ garlic and gingerroot (if not using the prepared minced versions)
- ✦ packaged sliced mushrooms
- ✦ cheese, including cream cheese and shredded cheese
- ✦ milk and cream, if not using packaged or frozen whipped topping

BASIC SPICES AND FLAVORINGS

The basic spices you'll need to create the recipes in this book are cayenne, ground cumin, ground cinnamon, dried Italian seasoning, cumin seeds, curry powder, hot pepper flakes, chili powder and ground ginger. You will also need vanilla and almond extract.

In addition, I recommend the use of sea salt rather than so-called table salt, and whole black peppercorns instead of ground black pepper. The taste of sea salt is far superior to that of table salt, which has an unpleasant acrid aftertaste. You can purchase fine-grain sea salt, which can be used as is, or the coarse crystals, which need to be ground in a salt mill before using. Black peppercorns have far more depth and flavor than previously ground black pepper, because the corns lose their aromatic oils immediately upon grinding. You'll need a good pepper mill to grind the corns. Make a point of testing pepper mills before you buy as many seem to be designed for appearance, not grinding ability. In my experience, you may have to pay a bit more for one that will do the job, but it will likely last for a decade or more.

THE SHOPPING PLAN

A plan designed to make it convenient to cook every day is built around the concept of shopping for groceries once a week. The idea is to stock up on the combination of fresh and processed foods that will get you through the next seven days. You can add plenty of variety to your diet by eating the most perishable items first. This includes fresh meat, poultry and fish, which should be cooked in the early part of the week. If these foods will not be used within two or three days (or before the expiration date), freeze them for later use. You'll still be able to make any of the delicious dishes in this book, such as Spicy Peanut Chicken, Chili con Carne Pronto, Crispy Shepherd's Pie or Paupiettes of Sole Florentine.

CONVENIENCE MEATS

Today, the food industry has taken convenience to new horizons with the introduction of many precooked meats like cooked, sliced chicken breasts and rotisserie chickens. This trend began years ago when consumers responded favorably to the then new offerings of more convenient cuts of meat, such as skinless, boneless chicken parts, and chicken or turkey cutlets. Ground meats and sausages, some of which have been around for centuries, are also part of the convenience tradition. These products cook quickly and require less prep work than many other types of meat. They also keep well if frozen. Just remember that using frozen meat requires advance planning. Packages should be thawed overnight in the refrigerator for dinnertime cooking the following day. Alternatively, you can use a microwave oven. Frozen meat takes about 7 minutes per pound to thaw on the Defrost setting. Pop the package in the microwave as soon as you walk through the door and it will likely be ready to cook when you are.

Stocking a good assortment of frozen fish and seafood is another technique for creating homemade taste in a matter of minutes. These products cook quickly and combine with a wide array of flavors and foods. Kept frozen, they have a long shelf life, enabling you to enjoy made-from-scratch taste using ingredients you're likely to have on hand. With the recipes in the book, you can quickly turn out tasty main courses such as Pan-Fried Halibut in Spicy Lemon Sauce, Creamy Corn and Shrimp or Potato Pancakes with Smoked Salmon any day of the week.

Keep a good supply of dried pasta and a selection of prepared ingredients on the shelf and you'll be able to have dishes such as Penne with Tuna and Peppers, Beans and Macaroni and Uptown Fettuccine Alfredo on the table in no time flat. Buy the freshest eggs you can find and combine them with canned or frozen vegetables for other outstanding midweek dinners, including Italian-Style Poached Eggs and Egg Foo Yung with Chinese Vegetables. Keep plenty of washed, bagged salad greens on hand, with an expiration date that extends beyond the week so you'll be able to enjoy a serving of healthy greens with dinner each night. Add some chopped onion, a sliced avocado (purchased while still firm, it will ripen by the time you're ready to eat it) and toss with your favorite dressing. And, with a good supply of non-perishable fruits in the freezer or on the shelf, you can quickly produce mouth-watering desserts such as Butterscotch Baked Peaches, Blueberry Buckle, Cherry Clafouti and Ginger Strawberry Fool.

FRESH VERSUS PREPARED

The decision to use a fresh ingredient rather than one with a prepared component is a personal one. Many people prefer to use frozen chopped onions, not only for convenience but because they find it painful to chop onions, which sting their eyes and make them sneeze. Some people are so in love with the taste of fresh lemons that they would never use bottled or frozen lemon juice. The same is true of bottled or frozen minced garlic and gingerroot. If you're the kind of person who always has fresh garlic and gingerroot on hand and doesn't mind adding a few extra minutes to the prep time of any recipe, by all means peel and chop your own. Similarly, squeeze your own lemon and lime juice. In addition to their time-saving qualities, the prepared versions of these ingredients also keep refrigerated for much longer than their fresh counterparts.

Appetizers, Snacks and Sandwiches

Every cook needs an abundant supply of versatile appetizer recipes. These tasty tidbits often do multiple duty — as starters to a sit-down meal, canapés for larger get-togethers, sandwich fillings, afternoon snacks and, on occasion, as the focus of a light meal. Sandwiches, which were one of the first convenience meals, are a great dish for casual dining and can often be retooled as canapés for entertaining. Stock a good selection of staples so you will be prepared to create delicious nibbles at the drop of a hat. Keep a loaf of ready-to-bake bread in the freezer or, if you have time, shop for the highest-quality and freshest bread the day you plan to use it.

Roasted Red Pepper Dip 16

Tunnato Spread................................. 17

Shrimp-Stuffed Avocado 18

Crab Louis..................................... 20

Smoked Oyster Hummus........................ 21

Tapenade...................................... 22

Egg and Olive Spread 24

Basil and White Bean Spread 25

Refried Nachos 26

Smoked Salmon and Red Caviar Mousse 28

Cheesy Anchovy Toasts 29

Sumptuous Chicken Sandwich with Brie.......... 30

Seafood on Toast 32

Tomato Rarebit 33

Pan Bagna 34

ON HAND

- ✓ Bottled roasted red peppers
- ✓ Prepared olive paste
- ✓ Prepared anchovy paste and/or preserved anchovies
- ✓ Canned or frozen crab
- ✓ Canned tuna, preferably Italian, packed in olive oil
- ✓ Smoked oysters
- ✓ Frozen smoked salmon
- ✓ Canned and marinated artichoke hearts
- ✓ Capers
- ✓ Fresh eggs
- ✓ Canned chickpeas
- ✓ Prepared pesto sauce (sun-dried tomato and basil)
- ✓ Crackers
- ✓ Green and/or black olives

◀ Roasted Red Pepper Dip and Tunnato Spread

Roasted Red Pepper Dip

Serve this tasty dip with crudités, crackers or pumpernickel rounds for an elegant appetizer. Great on its own, it also makes a flavorful addition to a tasting platter.

8 oz	feta cheese	250 g
2	roasted red peppers	2

MAKES ABOUT 1¾ CUPS (425 ML)

Start to finish: 5 minutes

1. In a food processor, combine cheese and peppers and process until smooth.

TIP: I like to make this with creamy feta cheese (about 26% M.F.) as the lower-fat versions tend to produce a drier dip. If your results seem dry, add 1 tsp (5 mL) or so of olive oil and give the mix a final pulse.

EASY EXTRA

✦ For a zestier version of this dip, add hot pepper sauce to taste before processing.

ROASTED RED PEPPERS

Bottled roasted red peppers are now widely available and make an excellent substitute for those that are freshly roasted. These sweet and slightly smoky delicacies add an instant burst of flavor to many dishes and make a visually appealing addition to an appetizer tray. For added interest, cut roasted red peppers into strips, then spread each strip with about 1 tsp (5 mL) Tunnato Spread (see recipe, page 17), roll up and secure with a toothpick.

To roast peppers: If you prefer to roast your own, place peppers under a preheated broiler. Broil, turning two or three times, until the skin is uniformly black, then place in a large bowl or a saucepan. Cover and let cool before lifting off the skins and removing the stems and seeds.

Tunnato Spread

Don't be fooled by the simplicity of this recipe: it is a mouth-watering combination. Amazingly versatile, this ambrosial mixture excels as a dip. Make it the centerpiece of a tasting platter, surrounded by celery sticks and cucumber slices or tender leaves of Belgian endive. It also performs well as a sauce for plated appetizers or salade composé (for which the ingredients are arranged on a plate rather than tossed together).

¾ cup	mayonnaise (see Tip, left)	175 mL
1	can (6 oz/170 g) tuna, preferably Italian, packed in olive oil, drained	1
20	parsley leaves	20
	Crudités (see below)	

MAKES ABOUT 1½ CUPS (375 ML)

Start to finish: 5 minutes

TIP: Don't confuse real mayonnaise with "mayonnaise-type" salad dressings, which are similar in appearance. Mayonnaise is a combination of egg yolks, vinegar or lemon juice, olive oil and seasonings. Imitators will contain additional ingredients, such as sugar, flour or milk. Make sure the label says mayonnaise and check the ingredients.

EASY EXTRAS

✦ Add 1 to 2 tbsp (15 to 25 mL) drained capers and/or 1 to 2 tbsp (15 to 25 mL) finely chopped green onions.

1. In a food processor, combine mayonnaise, tuna and parsley. Process until smooth.

2. Transfer to a small bowl and serve surrounded by crudités for dipping. If not using immediately, cover and refrigerate for up to 3 days.

VARIATIONS: Tunnato-Stuffed Eggs (Serves 6 to 8): Hard-cook 4 eggs (see page 55). Let cool and peel. Cut in half lengthwise. Pop out the yolks and mash with ¼ cup (50 mL) Tunnato Spread. Mound the mixture back into the whites. Dust with 1 tsp (5 mL) paprika, if desired. If you prefer a plated appetizer, simply cut the peeled cooked eggs in half, arrange them on a platter and spoon the sauce over top.

Asparagus with Tunnato (Serves 4): Arrange 1 can or jar (16 oz/330 g approx.) white asparagus, drained, on a small platter or serving plate. Top with ¼ cup (50 mL) Tunnato Spread. Use fresh green asparagus in season, if desired. You can also turn this into a salad by spreading a layer of salad greens over a large platter. Arrange the asparagus over the greens and top with Tunnato Spread.

CRUDITÉS

Crudités are cut-up vegetables used for dipping. Today, the selection of vegetables in the market – more and more of which are washed and precut – makes it convenient to use these healthful ingredients as crudités. Popular choices are broccoli and cauliflower florets, peeled baby carrots, Belgian endive and cherry tomatoes. And don't forget old standbys such as celery sticks and thinly sliced cucumber. One of my favorites is blanched Brussels sprouts, which are particularly good with strongly flavored dips.

Shrimp-Stuffed Avocado

I learned to make this "gourmet" appetizer while at university, and it has remained a favorite ever since. Depend upon avocados, one of nature's own convenience foods, for ease of preparation and the perfect combination of flavor and texture. This dish makes an elegant starter for any meal, and this quantity also makes a delicious and nutritious light dinner for two. Look for cooked salad shrimp at your supermarket fish counter.

SERVES 4

Start to finish: 10 minutes

TIP: Do not halve avocados until just before serving; otherwise the flesh will turn brown. Use the tip of a spoon to remove the pit.

EASY EXTRA

✦ Add 2 tbsp (25 mL) finely chopped dill along with the celery.

8 oz	cooked salad shrimp, thawed and drained if frozen, or 2 cans (each 3¾ oz/106 g) shrimp, rinsed and drained	250 g
1 tbsp	lemon juice	15 mL
½ cup	finely chopped celery	125 mL
2 tbsp	finely chopped green onion (white part only)	25 mL
¼ cup	mayonnaise	50 mL
	Salt and freshly ground black pepper	
2	avocados	2

1. In a bowl, combine shrimp and lemon juice. Toss to combine. Add celery, green onion, mayonnaise and salt and black pepper to taste. Mix well.

2. Cut each avocado in half and remove pits (see Tip, left).

3. Place one avocado half on each plate. Fill with shrimp mixture (it will spill over the sides) and serve immediately.

AVOCADOS

Rich, buttery avocados are one of my favorite convenience foods. When perfectly ripe, they are delicious with just a splash of Vinaigrette (see recipe, page 58). Sliced or chopped, they make a delightful addition to a plain green salad. They are high in unsaturated (healthy) fat and are loaded with nutrients. One word of caution: most of the avocados in supermarkets are still unripe and require another two or three days to ripen. Once home, keep them in a warm, dark place. You'll know they are ripe when they respond to the pressure of your finger. If you need to speed up the ripening process, place them in a brown paper bag with an apple or banana, which generates ethylene gas. Once ripe, avocados should be stored in the refrigerator.

Crab Louis

Louis sauce, which is basically a mixture of mayonnaise, chili sauce and other seasonings, is the basis for this recipe. Most often used to make Crab Louis, it is also delicious served over cold cooked shrimp or lobster. I like to use Crab Louis as a spread, with thin slices of cucumber, spears of Belgian endive, crackers or thinly sliced baguette. It also makes a spectacular salad or plated appetizer served over a bed of lettuce greens and garnished with hard-cooked eggs.

MAKES ABOUT
1⅓ CUPS (325 ML)

Start to finish: 10 minutes

EASY EXTRAS

✦ Add 2 tbsp (25 mL) finely diced green bell pepper along with the onion.

✦ Add a pinch of cayenne pepper.

2	cans (each 4 oz/125 g) crabmeat, drained, or 8 oz (250 g) crabmeat, thawed and drained if frozen	2
LOUIS SAUCE		
¾ cup	mayonnaise	175 mL
¼ cup	tomato-based chili sauce	50 mL
2 tbsp	lemon juice	25 mL
1 tbsp	finely chopped red or green onion	15 mL
1 tbsp	finely chopped parsley	15 mL
¼ tsp	Worcestershire sauce	1 mL
	Freshly ground black pepper	

1. *Louis Sauce:* In a bowl, combine mayonnaise, chili sauce, lemon juice, onion, parsley and Worcestershire sauce. Mix well.

2. Add crab and toss to combine. Season with black pepper to taste.

VARIATION: Even Easier Crab Louis: Substitute 1 cup (250 mL) prepared Thousand Islands salad dressing for the Louis Sauce. Proceed with Step 2.

ENHANCED MAYONNAISE

Louis Sauce is just one of many kinds of enhanced mayonnaise, such as Easy Tartar Sauce (see recipe, page 92) and Aïoli (see recipe below), that can be created in a flash and used to dress up plain ingredients.

Aïoli: This garlic-flavored mayonnaise can anchor a tasting platter, surrounded by hard-cooked eggs, boiled new potatoes, blanched green beans, cauliflower or broccoli florets. I especially enjoy aïoli with shrimp, one of my family's favorite hot-weather dinners. We barbecue large shrimp in their shells, peel them at the table and dip them into the aïoli. Accompaniments are basic: a crisp green or fresh tomato salad, crusty bread and ice cold Alsatian Gewurztraminer, a fruity white wine.

To make Aïoli: Combine 1 cup (250 mL) mayonnaise with 2 tbsp (25 mL) minced garlic. Stir to blend.

Smoked Oyster Hummus

Served on its own or as a focus of a tasting platter, this intriguing spread, which is a variation on traditional Middle Eastern hummus, always gets rave reviews. Accompany with pita bread, pita toasts, crackers or crudités, such as celery sticks, peeled baby carrots or sliced cucumbers.

¼ cup	lemon juice	50 mL
¼ cup	olive oil	50 mL
1	large roasted red pepper (see page 16)	1
1 tbsp	minced garlic	15 mL
½ tsp	salt	2 mL
1	can (19 oz/540 mL) chickpeas, drained and rinsed	1
1	can (3 oz/90 g) smoked oysters, drained	1
	Freshly ground black pepper	

MAKES ABOUT 3 CUPS (750 ML)

Start to finish: 10 minutes

TIP: Taste the oysters before using to ensure their flavor meets your approval, as it can vary from brand to brand, affecting the result.

1. In a food processor, combine lemon juice, olive oil, roasted red pepper, garlic and salt. Process until smooth.
2. Add chickpeas and process until mixture is still a little chunky but well blended. Add oysters and process until just combined. Season with black pepper to taste.

VARIATION: Hummus with Tahini: Substitute ½ cup (125 mL) tahini (sesame seed paste) for the smoked oysters.

BISCUITS AND BREADS

When choosing biscuits or crackers for dips and spreads, look for high-quality versions that don't have strong flavors or too much salt. Pita bread or crisps, flatbreads, bread sticks, thinly sliced pumpernickel and Crostini (see recipe, page 29) go well with specific recipes. And you can rarely go wrong with a fresh baguette.

GERMANTOWN COMMUNITY LIBRARY
GERMANTOWN, WI 53022

Tapenade

Known as Provençal caviar, tapenade is a flavorful mixture of capers, olives and anchovies, among other ingredients. Although it is tasty, it can be heavy, so I prefer this lighter version, which has added tuna. I like to serve this with carrot or celery sticks, sliced cucumber, crackers or crostini. It also makes a delicious filling for hard-cooked eggs (see Variation, right).

MAKES ABOUT
¾ CUP (175 ML)

Start to finish: 10 minutes

EASY EXTRA

✦ Add 1 chopped roasted red pepper along with the tuna.

1	can (6 oz/170 g) tuna, preferably Italian, packed in olive oil, drained	1
4	anchovies	4
2 tbsp	drained capers	25 mL
1 tbsp	lemon juice	15 mL
1 tsp	minced garlic	5 mL
10	pitted black olives	10
¼ cup	olive oil	50 mL

1. In a food processor, combine tuna, anchovies, capers, lemon juice, garlic and olives. Process until ingredients are combined but still chunky. Add olive oil and pulse until blended. Spoon into a bowl, cover tightly and refrigerate until ready to use.

VARIATION: Tapenade-Stuffed Eggs: Hard-cook eggs (see page 55). Let cool and peel. Cut in half lengthwise. Pop out the yolks and add 1 tsp (5 mL) tapenade per yolk. Mash together and use this mixture to fill the whites. Dust with paprika, if desired.

ANCHOVIES

Always have some preserved anchovies in the refrigerator as they are a great enhancement to many dishes. I prefer to buy anchovies in a jar, rather than a tin, as it allows me to use only the quantity I require. While anchovies are great flavor boosters, they are also a handy convenience food on their own. For instance, all it takes is a food processor, plain cream cheese and anchovies to make this tasty anchovy spread.

Anchovy Spread: Simply process anchovies and cream cheese in a food processor until smooth. Use one anchovy fillet per ounce (30 g) of cream cheese. If you prefer a milder or more pungent result, adjust accordingly. For variety, try adding 1 tbsp (15 mL) sun-dried tomato pesto to every 4 oz (125 g) cream cheese. Serve on Belgian endive spears and/or thin slices of cucumber or baguette.

Egg and Olive Spread

It's easy to overlook old-fashioned egg salad as an appetizing hors d'oeuvre, likely because it is such a common filling for sandwiches. But it's a classic for a reason: it tastes good and appeals to a wide variety of people. Initially surprised, guests are always delighted when I serve this with a plate of pumpernickel rounds or dark rye bread, and it quickly disappears. On the rare occasion when there are leftovers, they get recycled into a lunchtime sandwich.

4	hard-cooked eggs (see page 55), peeled and chopped	4
2 tbsp	mayonnaise	25 mL
6	pimento-stuffed green olives, finely chopped	6
	Salt and freshly ground black pepper	
	Pumpernickel rounds or dark rye bread	

1. In a bowl, combine eggs, mayonnaise and olives. Mix well. Season with salt and black pepper to taste.

2. Using an ice cream scoop, mound into a small serving bowl. Accompany with pumpernickel rounds or dark rye bread.

VARIATIONS: Egg and Chive Spread: Substitute 1 tbsp (15 mL) finely chopped chives for the olives.

Egg and Roasted Red Pepper Spread: Substitute 2 small roasted red peppers, finely chopped, for the olives.

Egg and Black Olive Crostini: Spread each Crostini (see recipe, page 29) with 1 tsp (5 mL) black olive paste and top with Egg and Roasted Red Pepper Spread.

Savory Egg Salad Sandwich: Spread the filling between two slices of lightly buttered bread, preferably dark rye.

MAKES ABOUT
1 1/2 CUPS (375 ML)

Start to finish: 25 minutes (with cooking eggs)

TIP: Olive paste is available in the deli section of many supermarkets.

EASY EXTRA

✦ Dust lightly with paprika.

THE TASTING PLATTER

Call them what you will — tapas in Spain, mezes in Greece and antipasti in Italy — but the idea of "grazing" from appetizing platters filled with tasty nibbles has changed the way we eat. Using a selection of prepared foods and two or three recipes in this chapter, you can quickly create a tasting platter to rival more labor-intensive versions. Serve one or two of the dips or spreads in small bowls and surround with appropriate dippers such as crudités (see page 17). If desired, add a larger bowl containing a chilled marinated salad (see Salads). Add some good olives, a bit of cheese, and crackers or fresh baguette and wait for the compliments.

Basil and White Bean Spread

Don't tell and no one will ever guess how easy it is to make this delicious and sophisticated spread. I like to serve this with Crostini (see recipe, page 29) brushed with garlic-infused olive oil (see Tips, below), but sliced baguette and crackers work well, too.

**MAKES ABOUT
3 CUPS (750 ML)**

Start to finish: 10 minutes

TIPS: Make sure you have thoroughly dried the parsley (patting between layers of paper towel) before adding to the food processor; otherwise the spread may be watery.

You can purchase garlic-infused olive oil, but it is easy to make your own – just be sure to use it immediately as infused oils are a favored medium for bacteria growth. *Garlic-Infused Olive Oil:* In a clean jar or cruet, combine ¼ cup (50 mL) olive oil and 1 tbsp (15 mL) minced garlic. Cover and let steep at room temperature for several hours. Strain through a fine sieve or funnel lined with a paper coffee filter. Discard garlic.

1	can (19 oz/540 mL) white kidney beans, drained and rinsed	1
2 cups	packed flat-leaf parsley leaves (see Tips, left)	500 mL
2 tbsp	prepared basil pesto sauce	25 mL
1 tbsp	minced garlic	15 mL
1 tbsp	lemon juice	15 mL
	Salt and freshly ground black pepper	

1. In a food processor, combine beans, parsley, basil pesto, garlic and lemon juice. Process until smooth. Season with salt and black pepper to taste.

BEAN CUISINE

Canned and frozen beans are a great convenience food. Highly nutritious, they blend well with a wide variety of flavors and are extremely versatile. There are many types of beans, and new and exotic varieties, such as edamame (soybeans), are constantly turning up on supermarket shelves. A staple of Japanese cuisine, edamame, which have a crispy texture and mild nutty flavor, make a delicious appetizer or snack. Buy them frozen or cooked, in or out of the pod. Serve shelled edamame (thaw if frozen) simply, in a bowl. For informal gatherings, serve edamame in their shells and provide bowls for the residue. But be warned – edamame are addictive.

Refried Nachos

A favorite of teenagers, nachos are also a great comfort food dish. In this recipe, the degree of spice depends upon the heat of the salsa. If you are heat averse, use a mild salsa. If you are a heat seeker, use a spicy one.

1	can (14 oz/398 mL) refried beans	1
1 cup	prepared salsa	250 mL
1	can (4.5 oz/127 mL) chopped green chilies, drained	1
2 cups	shredded Cheddar or Monterey Jack cheese	500 mL
	Tortilla chips or tostadas	

MAKES ABOUT 4 CUPS (1 L)

Start to finish: 10 minutes

TIP: To microwave, place beans, salsa and chilies in a microwave-safe dish. Microwave on High until bubbling, about 4 minutes. Stir in cheese and microwave until melted, about 1½ minutes.

EASY EXTRAS

✦ To jack up the heat, add a finely chopped jalapeño pepper along with the beans.

✦ If you like a hint of smoke as well as heat, add a finely chopped chipotle pepper in adobo sauce.

1. In a saucepan over medium heat, bring beans, salsa and chilies to a boil. (You can also do this in the microwave; see Tip, left.) Stir in cheese until melted. Serve with tortilla chips or tostadas for dipping.

VARIATIONS: Mexican Pita Pizzas: Place pita breads in a large baking dish and spread with nacho mixture. Bake in 400°F (200°C) oven until the mixture is hot and bubbling, about 10 minutes. Serve with a knife and fork.

Bean Tacos: Warm 4 to 6 taco shells according to package directions. Fill with bean mixture and garnish with any combination of lettuce, tomato, green or red onion, avocado and/or sour cream.

Smoked Salmon and Red Caviar Mousse

This is one of my favorite preambles to a dinner party. I've been making it for years because it's so easy to prepare yet elegant enough to start the most sophisticated meal. I love the sensation when the lumpfish caviar bursts on my tongue. Serve on thinly sliced baguette, plain biscuits or cocktail-size slices of dark rye bread.

MAKES ABOUT 2 CUPS (500 ML)

Start to finish: 10 minutes

TIP: The quantity of cream required depends upon the kind of smoked salmon you are using. You may need more cream if using wild salmon, which is likely to have a heavier texture than the farmed variety. The mousse mixture should be light enough to fold in the red caviar without appearing to crush the delicate roe.

8 oz	smoked salmon	250 g
½ to ¾ cup	whipping (35%) cream (see Tip, left)	125 to 175 mL
1 tbsp	lemon juice	15 mL
2 tbsp	red lumpfish roe	25 mL
	Freshly ground black pepper	

1. In a food processor, combine smoked salmon, cream and lemon juice. Process until smooth. Fold in lumpfish roe. Season with black pepper to taste. Spoon into a serving bowl. Refrigerate until ready to serve.

SMOKED SALMON

You can purchase high-quality frozen smoked salmon in many supermarkets. I always have a package or two in the freezer as it's an easy way to quickly create a special dish. Add a few slices to Best-Ever Scrambled Eggs (see recipe, page 75) or use it to top freshly made Potato Pancakes (see recipe, page 94) for a delicious brunch or light dinner. Save any leftovers to chop finely and sprinkle over a steaming bowl of Creamy Cauliflower Soup (see recipe, page 44).

Cheesy Anchovy Toasts

This is one of my favorite hot canapés. The pungent anchovies are a perfect complement to the strong taste of smoked mozzarella. For convenience, prepare the crostini ahead of time and heat under the broiler in a preheated (350°F/180°C) oven for a minute or two.

MAKES 8 CROSTINI

Start to finish: 10 minutes

TIPS: If you don't have a baguette, make this dish using toast triangles. Just toast sliced white bread, remove the crusts, then cut each slice into 4 triangles. Proceed with Step 2.

Smoked mozzarella is available in the deli section of many supermarkets.

If you don't have anchovy paste, you can make this recipe using anchovy fillets. For this quantity, finely chop 8 anchovy fillets. Combine in a saucepan with 1 tsp (5 mL) minced garlic and 2 tbsp (25 mL) olive oil. Heat over low heat, stirring occasionally, until the anchovies dissolve. Spoon about $\frac{1}{2}$ tsp (2 mL) onto each crostini, then top with cheese.

✦ PREHEAT BROILER

CROSTINI

8	slices baguette (each $\frac{1}{4}$ inch/0.5 cm thick) Olive oil	8
8 tsp	anchovy paste (see Tips, left)	40 mL
4 oz	smoked mozzarella cheese, thinly sliced	125 g

1. *Crostini:* Brush baguette slices lightly with olive oil on both sides. Place under preheated broiler and toast until golden, turning once, about 2 minutes per side.

2. Spread each crostini with 1 tsp (5 mL) anchovy paste. Top with mozzarella slice. Place under preheated broiler and heat until cheese is melted, about 2 minutes. Serve piping hot.

ANCHOVY PASTE

Anchovy paste is available in the refrigerated section of most supermarkets. It is a handy way to add bite to many dishes, particularly those featuring tomatoes. As a rule of thumb, substitute about 1 tsp (5 mL) anchovy paste for each anchovy called for in the recipe.

Sumptuous Chicken Sandwich with Brie

This sandwich is so spectacular that no one will believe how easy it is to make.

SERVES 4

Start to finish: 15 minutes

TIP: It is difficult to give accurate times for procedures done under the broiler because results are affected not only by the distance between the food and the heat but also by the temperature of the broiler, which varies dramatically among ovens. The times I have suggested are based on placing the food 2 inches (5 cm) from the element. They are at the low end of the spectrum, so you may find it takes you longer to produce the desired result. However, when using a broiler, it is always a good idea to keep a close eye on food as it can burn quickly.

✦ PREHEAT BROILER

2 tbsp	mayonnaise	25 mL
2 tbsp	prepared sun-dried tomato pesto	25 mL
1 tsp	Dijon mustard	5 mL
¼ tsp	salt	1 mL
	Freshly ground black pepper	
2 cups	cubed (½ inch/1 cm) cooked chicken	500 mL
4	onion or Kaiser buns, halved	4
8 oz	Brie cheese, thinly sliced	250 g
	Lettuce (optional)	
	Sliced tomato (optional)	

1. In a bowl, combine mayonnaise, pesto, mustard, salt, and black pepper to taste. Stir until blended. Add chicken and toss to combine.

2. Spread bottom halves of buns with equal portions of chicken mixture. Lay cheese slices across top halves. Place tops on a baking sheet and broil until cheese is just beginning to melt and run over the sides of the bun, about 2 minutes. Garnish with lettuce and tomatoes, if desired. Unite with bottoms, cut in half and serve.

Seafood on Toast

This is a great luncheon dish and an excellent way to use up any Alfredo sauce you may have left over from another recipe. Double or triple the quantity, if desired.

SERVES 2

Start to finish: 10 minutes

EASY EXTRAS

✦ Add 2 tbsp (25 mL) finely chopped red or green bell pepper or roasted red pepper along with the crab.

✦ Garnish with finely chopped green onion or parsley to taste.

1	can (6 oz/170 g) crabmeat, lobster or shrimp, drained	1
1/2 cup	prepared Alfredo sauce	125 mL
2 tbsp	prepared sun-dried tomato pesto	25 mL
2 tsp	lemon juice	10 mL
	Freshly ground black pepper	
2	slices toast	2

1. In a small saucepan over low heat, combine crab, Alfredo sauce, pesto and lemon juice. Heat until barely simmering, about 3 minutes. Season with black pepper to taste.

2. Spoon over warm toast and serve immediately.

MAXIMIZE CONVENIENCE
BY USING:
✦ Prepared Alfredo sauce
✦ Prepared pesto sauce
✦ Bottled or frozen lemon juice

Tomato Rarebit

Here's a delicious solution to what to do with leftover canned tomatoes. Double or triple the quantity, as desired.

SERVES 2

Start to finish: 10 minutes

1 cup	drained canned tomatoes, coarsely chopped	250 mL
1 tsp	Worcestershire sauce	5 mL
1 tsp	Dijon mustard	5 mL
1 cup	shredded Cheddar cheese	250 mL
	Salt and freshly ground black pepper	
2	slices (or more) toast	2

1. In a small saucepan over medium heat, combine tomatoes, Worcestershire sauce and Dijon mustard. Bring to a boil.

2. Reduce heat to low. Add cheese and cook, stirring, until melted. Season with salt and black pepper to taste. Spoon over warm toast and serve.

GREAT GRILLED CHEESE SANDWICH

One of my favorite comfort food lunches is a bowl of homemade Classic Cream of Tomato Soup (see recipe, page 50) and a hot grilled cheese sandwich. Here's my recipe for the sandwich. Spread the inside of one slice of bread with sun-dried tomato pesto. Layer on thinly sliced Cheddar cheese to taste. Top with a second slice of bread and spread the outside portion with softened butter. Heat a skillet over medium heat. Add the sandwich, buttered side down, and cook until it browns and the cheese begins to melt. Spread softened butter over the top of the sandwich. Turn and cook until the remaining side is browned and the cheese is melted.

Pan Bagna

Packed in a cooler, this Provençal-style sandwich is my favorite picnic staple. However, it also does extra duty as an easy make-ahead tidbit for a tasting platter or canapé tray. At our house, it gets most use as the best-ever filling for a tuna sandwich.

SERVES 4 AS A SANDWICH OR 8 TO 10 AS A CANAPÉ

Start to finish: 15 minutes
Chilling: 4 hours

EASY EXTRAS

✦ Add 1 to 2 tsp (5 to 10 mL) finely chopped bottled hot banana peppers and/or 1 tsp (5 mL) drained capers to mixture.

1	can (6 oz/170 g) flaked white tuna, drained	1
2 tbsp	each finely chopped red or green onion, celery, parsley, roasted red pepper and pitted black olives (use all or some of the above, depending upon what you have on hand)	25 mL
2 tbsp	mayonnaise	25 mL
1 tbsp	lemon juice	15 mL
1 tbsp	olive oil	15 mL
½ tsp	salt	2 mL
	Freshly ground black pepper	
1	baguette, hero loaf or 4 crusty rolls, split lengthwise	1

1. In a bowl, combine tuna, vegetables, mayonnaise, lemon juice, olive oil, salt, and black pepper to taste. Mix well.

2. Spread mixture evenly over bottom half of baguette. Cover with the top portion and cut in half. Press down firmly on each piece, then wrap tightly in plastic wrap. Place in a pan and cover with a heavy weight (I have a foil-wrapped brick that I keep for this purpose). Refrigerate for 4 hours or overnight.

3. To serve as a sandwich, cut each baguette piece in half. To serve as a canapé, cut each piece into 4 or 5 slices.

VARIATION: The World's Best Tuna Sandwich: Spread the filling over your favorite bread and serve immediately.

Soups

Nothing says comfort like a bowl of steaming soup. One of our most basic dishes, soup is a great lunchtime dish and an always welcome first course. Heartier versions such as chowders are a meal in a bowl. Although there are many tasty canned soups on the market, soup is one of the easiest and most foolproof dishes to make yourself, and you can quickly turn out delicious homemade soups using ingredients you're likely to have on hand.

Squash and White Bean Soup with Basil Pesto.... 38

Corn Chowder 39

Broccoli and Cheddar Cheese Soup.............. 40

Chili Cheddar Soup 42

Ginger Chili Sweet Potato Soup.................. 43

Creamy Cauliflower Soup 44

Borscht 46

Lemony Lentil Soup with Spinach 47

Sweet Green Pea Soup 48

Classic Cream of Tomato Soup 50

New England Clam Chowder...................... 51

ON HAND

- ✓ Prepared stock (beef, chicken, vegetable)
- ✓ Canned Cheddar cheese soup
- ✓ Bottled roasted red peppers
- ✓ Canned clams
- ✓ Selection of canned vegetables, such as tomatoes, potatoes, beets, legumes, sweet potatoes and corn
- ✓ Selection of frozen vegetables, such as peas, diced onions, squash, broccoli and cauliflower florets
- ✓ Cheddar cheese
- ✓ Worcestershire sauce
- ✓ Prepared pesto sauce (sun-dried tomato and basil)

◄ Squash and White Bean Soup with Basil Pesto

Squash and White Bean Soup with Basil Pesto

This nutritious soup takes advantage of basil pesto sauce and white beans, a Tuscan favorite, to add Italian flair to a simple recipe. Serve this with salad for a light meal or in smaller amounts for a first course to a more elaborate dinner.

SERVES 4

Start to finish: 25 minutes

TIP: If you prefer a smoother soup and a more elegant presentation, purée mixture and reheat before ladling into bowls. Drizzle pesto over the soup when it is in the bowl.

EASY EXTRAS

✦ Add 1 cup (250 mL) chopped red bell pepper or frozen mixed bell pepper strips along with the garlic.

✦ Add 2 cherry tomatoes, halved, to each bowl of soup after stirring in the pesto.

✦ Sprinkle each serving with grated Parmesan cheese.

1 tbsp	vegetable oil	15 mL
1 cup	diced onion	250 mL
1 tbsp	minced garlic	15 mL
1/2 tsp	salt	2 mL
	Freshly ground black pepper	
2 cups	diced butternut squash	500 mL
1	can (19 oz/540 mL) white kidney or navy beans, drained and rinsed	1
3 cups	vegetable or chicken stock	750 mL
1/4 cup	prepared basil pesto sauce	50 mL

1. In a large saucepan, heat oil over medium heat. Add onion and cook, stirring, until softened, about 3 minutes. Add garlic, salt, and black pepper to taste. Cook, stirring, for 1 minute.

2. Add squash, beans and stock. Bring to a boil. Reduce heat to low and simmer for 15 minutes.

3. Ladle soup into 4 bowls. Add 1 tbsp (15 mL) basil pesto to each bowl and stir gently to create ribbon effect.

MAXIMIZE CONVENIENCE BY USING:

✦ Frozen diced onion
✦ Bottled or frozen minced garlic
✦ Frozen diced butternut squash
✦ Already grated Parmesan cheese

Corn Chowder

A steaming bowl of hearty chowder served with crusty rolls is one of my favorite light meals. This version, made with corn rather than traditional clams, is sweet and flavorful.

SERVES 4

Start to finish: 25 minutes

TIP: An easy way to get the required quantity of stock for this recipe is to pour 1 can (10 oz/284 mL) condensed broth into a 4-cup (1 L) measure. Add water to reach the 3-cup (750 mL) measure.

EASY EXTRAS

+ If you prefer a creamier chowder, stir in ¹/₂ cup (125 mL) whipping (35%) or table (18%) cream before serving and simmer until heated through.

+ Add 2 tbsp (25 mL) precooked bacon pieces or 2 slices crisp cooked bacon, crumbled, along with the Italian seasoning.

+ Add hot pepper sauce to taste just before serving.

2 tbsp	butter	25 mL
1 cup	diced onion	250 mL
1 tsp	dried Italian seasoning	5 mL
¹/₂ tsp	salt	2 mL
	Freshly ground black pepper	
2	cans (each 14 oz/398 mL) cream-style corn	2
1	can (19 oz/540 mL) whole white potatoes, drained and chopped, or 2 cups (500 mL) cubed cooked potatoes	1
3 cups	chicken or vegetable stock	750 mL
1 tsp	Worcestershire sauce	5 mL

1. In a large saucepan, melt butter over medium heat. Add onion and cook, stirring, until softened, about 3 minutes. Add Italian seasoning, salt, and black pepper to taste. Cook, stirring, for 1 minute.

2. Add corn, potatoes, chicken stock and Worcestershire sauce. Bring to a boil. Reduce heat to low and simmer for 15 minutes. Ladle into bowls and serve piping hot.

> **STOCK**
>
> The flavored liquid that results when meat and/or vegetables are cooked in water and strained (often referred to as broth) is key to making tasty soup. There are many excellent prepared stocks on the market today, and it is wise to sample a selection and choose those that suit your taste. The most common form is condensed broth sold in a 10-oz (284 mL) can. If a recipe calls for 3 cups (750 mL) stock, just add water to a can of condensed broth to reach the required amount. When purchasing stock that is frozen or in jars or Tetra packs, check the label. Most of these brands are ready to use and do not require the addition of water.

Broccoli and Cheddar Cheese Soup

I love the rich Cheddar taste of this hearty soup. Serve smaller portions as a prelude to a traditional roast beef dinner or add a salad and crusty bread for a nutritious light meal.

SERVES 4

Start to finish: 30 minutes

TIPS: Taste before serving and add salt if needed.

If you don't have vegetable or chicken stock, use 3 cups (750 mL) water instead.

EASY EXTRA

✦ For a hit of heat, add hot pepper sauce to taste, just before serving.

1 tbsp	vegetable oil	15 mL
1 cup	diced onion	250 mL
1 tbsp	minced garlic	15 mL
Pinch	cayenne pepper	Pinch
	Freshly ground black pepper	
1	can (10 oz/284 mL) condensed Cheddar cheese soup, undiluted	1
1 tbsp	Dijon mustard	15 mL
3 cups	vegetable or chicken stock	750 mL
4 cups	broccoli florets	1 L
2 cups	shredded Cheddar cheese	500 mL

1. In a large saucepan, heat oil over medium heat. Add onion and cook, stirring, until softened, about 3 minutes. Add garlic, cayenne, and black pepper to taste. Cook, stirring, for 1 minute.

2. Add soup and mustard, stirring until smooth. Gradually stir in stock. Add broccoli and bring to a boil. Reduce heat to low and simmer until broccoli is tender, about 10 minutes.

3. Using a slotted spoon, transfer solids to a food processor or blender. Add $\frac{1}{2}$ cup (125 mL) of the cooking liquid and process until smooth. (You can also do this in the saucepan, using a hand-held blender.)

4. Return mixture to saucepan over low heat. Add Cheddar cheese and stir until smooth, being careful not to let the mixture boil. Serve piping hot.

MAXIMIZE CONVENIENCE
BY USING:
✦ Bottled or frozen minced garlic
✦ Prepared stock
✦ Frozen or precut fresh broccoli florets
✦ Already shredded Cheddar cheese

Chili Cheddar Soup

This delicious and hearty soup is a meal in a bowl. Made with vegetable stock, it is suitable for vegetarians. My family enjoys this for a light weeknight dinner, accompanied by hot crusty rolls and a simple green salad.

SERVES 4

Start to finish: 25 minutes

TIPS: If using fresh diced carrots, add along with the onion.

Taste before serving and add salt if needed.

Purée the soup in the saucepan using a hand-held blender.

EASY EXTRA

✦ For a spicier result, add 1 or 2 finely chopped jalapeño peppers along with the black pepper.

1 tbsp	butter	15 mL
1 cup	diced onion	250 mL
	Freshly ground black pepper	
1	can (10 oz/284 mL) condensed Cheddar cheese soup, undiluted	1
4 cups	vegetable or chicken stock	1 L
1	can (19 oz/540 mL) sliced new potatoes, drained, or 2 cups (500 mL) cubed cooked potatoes	1
1	can (14 oz/398 mL) carrots, drained, or 1 cup (250 mL) diced carrots (see Tips, left)	1
1	can (4.5 oz/127 mL) mild green chilies, drained (optional)	1
1 cup	shredded Cheddar cheese	250 mL

1. In a large saucepan, melt butter over medium heat. Add onion and cook, stirring, until softened, about 3 minutes. Add black pepper to taste.

2. Stir in soup until smooth. Gradually add stock, stirring until smooth. Add potatoes, carrots and chilies. Bring to a boil. Reduce heat to low and simmer for 10 minutes.

3. Using a slotted spoon, transfer solids to a food processor or blender. Add 1/2 cup (125 mL) of the cooking liquid and process until smooth.

4. Return mixture to saucepan over low heat. Add Cheddar cheese and cook, stirring, until melted, being careful not to let the mixture boil.

POTATOES

In addition to being the most versatile vegetable, potatoes can be used to add flavor and thickness to soups with less fat and fewer calories than traditional cream. However, the need to peel potatoes and their relatively long cooking time is a handicap to convenience. This is easily overcome by using canned potatoes.

Ginger Chile Sweet Potato Soup

This delicious soup features an intriguing combination of flavors. Hearty yet elegant, it makes a great prelude to a meal or a light dinner, accompanied by salad. Made with vegetable stock, it is suitable for vegetarians.

SERVES 4

Start to finish: 25 minutes

TIPS: One chopped roasted red pepper makes about 1 cup (125 mL).

Purée the soup in the saucepan using a hand-held blander.

EASY EXTRA

✦ Garnish with roasted red pepper strips just before serving.

1 tbsp	vegetable oil	15 mL
1 cup	diced onion	250 mL
1 tbsp	each minced garlic and gingerroot	15 mL
1 tbsp	chili powder	15 mL
½ tsp	salt	2 mL
	Freshly ground black pepper	
1	can (19 oz/540 mL) sweet potatoes, drained	1
1 cup	corn kernels, drained if canned or thawed if frozen	250 mL
3 cups	vegetable or chicken stock	750 mL
1	roasted red pepper, chopped	1
1 tbsp	lemon juice	15 mL

1. In a large saucepan, heat oil over medium heat. Add onion and cook, stirring, until softened, about 3 minutes. Add garlic, ginger, chili powder, salt, and black pepper to taste and cook, stirring, for 1 minute. Add sweet potatoes, corn kernels and stock. Bring to a boil. Reduce heat to low and simmer for 10 minutes. Stir in red pepper.

2. Using a slotted spoon, transfer solids to a food processor or blender. Add ½ cup (125 mL) of the cooking liquid and process until smooth. Return mixture to saucepan and stir in lemon juice. Ladle into bowls and serve immediately.

MAXIMIZE CONVENIENCE
BY USING:
✦ Frozen diced onions
✦ Bottled or frozen minced garlic
✦ Bottled minced gingerroot
✦ Bottled roasted red peppers
✦ Prepared stock
✦ Bottled or frozen lemon juice

Creamy Cauliflower Soup

One of the things I like about this soup is that it is delicious in its basic version but can easily be dressed up for special occasions (try the Smoked Salmon variation below). It reheats well, so there is no need to be concerned about the larger quantity if you are serving fewer people.

SERVES 6

Start to finish: 25 minutes

TIP: Use frozen cauliflower florets and/or diced onion in this recipe for convenience. If you run out, 1 medium onion produces about 1 cup (250 mL) diced onion.

EASY EXTRA

✦ For a hint of celery flavor, add ¼ tsp (1 mL) celery seed along with the black pepper.

2 tbsp	butter	25 mL
1 cup	diced onion (see Tip, left)	250 mL
1 tsp	salt	5 mL
	Freshly ground black pepper	
1	can (19 oz/540 mL) sliced potatoes, drained, or 2 cups (500 mL) chopped cooked potatoes	1
4 cups	cauliflower florets (see Tip, left)	1 L
6 cups	vegetable or chicken stock	1.5 L
½ cup	whipping (35%) cream	125 mL
2 tbsp	prepared sun-dried tomato pesto	25 mL

1. In a large saucepan, melt butter over medium heat. Add onion and cook, stirring, until softened, about 3 minutes. Add salt, and black pepper to taste, and cook, stirring, for 1 minute.

2. Add potatoes, cauliflower and stock. Bring to a boil. Reduce heat to low. Cover and cook until cauliflower is tender and flavors are combined, about 15 minutes.

3. Using a slotted spoon, transfer solids to a food processor or blender. Add ½ cup (125 mL) of the cooking liquid and process until smooth. (You can also do this in the saucepan, using a hand-held blender.)

4. Return mixture to saucepan over low heat. Add cream and pesto and heat gently until mixture almost reaches a simmer. Ladle into bowls and serve immediately.

VARIATIONS: Mulligatawny Soup: Add 1 tbsp (15 mL) curry powder along with the salt. Eliminate the pesto and stir in 2 cups (500 mL) chopped cooked chicken and/or ¼ cup (50 mL) mango chutney along with the cream.

Creamy Cauliflower Soup with Smoked Salmon: Garnish the finished soup with 2 oz (60 g) chopped smoked salmon and, if desired, 2 tbsp (25 mL) chopped green onion, chives or dill.

Borscht

Borscht is one of those hearty peasant soups that has transcended its origins. Here's an easy-to-make version that eliminates the unpleasant job of peeling beets. The baby spinach adds a pleasant note of freshness, which is sometimes provided by the addition of beet leaves in traditional recipes. Serve hot or cold with plenty of dark rye bread.

SERVES 4

Start to finish: 25 minutes

TIP: You can also use prepared beef, chicken or vegetable stock in this recipe. If it is not concentrated, use 2 cups (500 mL) stock and omit the water.

EASY EXTRA

✦ Top individual servings with a dollop of sour cream and/or finely chopped dill.

1 tbsp	vegetable oil	15 mL
1 cup	diced onion	250 mL
1 tbsp	minced garlic	15 mL
1	can (14 oz/398 mL) beets, including juice	1
1	can (10 oz/284 mL) condensed beef or chicken broth (see Tip, left)	1
½ cup	water	125 mL
½	bag (10 oz/300 g) washed baby spinach or 2 cups (500 mL) tightly packed washed baby spinach	½
2 tbsp	lemon juice	25 mL
	Salt and freshly ground black pepper	

1. In a large saucepan, heat oil over medium heat. Add onion and cook, stirring, until softened, about 3 minutes. Add garlic and cook, stirring, for 1 minute.

2. Add beets with juice, broth and water. Bring to a boil. Reduce heat to low and simmer for 10 minutes to combine flavors. Add spinach and cook, stirring, just until wilted. Stir in lemon juice. Season with salt and black pepper to taste.

3. Using a slotted spoon, transfer solids plus ½ cup (125 mL) of the liquid to a food processor or blender. Process until smooth. (You can also do this in the saucepan, using a hand-held blender.)

4. Return mixture to saucepan and stir to blend. Serve hot or chill thoroughly.

MAXIMIZE CONVENIENCE BY USING:
✦ Frozen diced onions
✦ Bottled minced garlic
✦ Washed baby spinach
✦ Bottled or frozen lemon juice

Lemony Lentil Soup with Spinach

This soup is so light and refreshing it's hard to believe that it's also packed with nutrition.

SERVES 4

Start to finish: 25 minutes

TIP: If you prefer, use 1 cup (250 mL) dried brown lentils, cooked, instead of the canned. Thoroughly rinse lentils under cold running water, then place in a large saucepan. Cover with 3 cups (750 mL) cold water. Bring to a boil over medium heat. Reduce heat to low and simmer until tender, about 25 minutes. Drain.

EASY EXTRA

✦ For a more lemony flavor, add 1 tsp (5 mL) grated lemon zest along with the garlic.

1 tbsp	vegetable oil	15 mL
1 cup	diced onion	250 mL
1 tbsp	minced garlic	15 mL
Pinch	cayenne pepper	Pinch
	Freshly ground black pepper	
1	package (10 oz/300 g) frozen chopped spinach or 1 bag (10 oz/300 g) fresh spinach, stems removed and chopped	1
1	can (19 oz/540 mL) lentils, drained and rinsed	1
5 cups	vegetable or chicken stock	1.25 L
1/4 cup	lemon juice	50 mL
	Salt	

1. In a large saucepan, heat oil over medium heat. Add onion and cook, stirring, until softened, about 3 minutes. Add garlic, cayenne, and black pepper to taste. Cook, stirring, for 1 minute.

2. Add spinach and cook, stirring and breaking up with spoon, until thawed (if frozen) or wilted (if fresh). Add lentils and stock. Bring to a boil. Reduce heat to low and simmer for 15 minutes to cook spinach and combine flavors. Stir in lemon juice, and salt to taste. Serve immediately.

VARIATION: Curried Lentil and Spinach Soup: Add 1 tsp (5 mL) to 1 tbsp (15 mL) curry powder, depending upon the degree of spice you prefer, along with the garlic.

Sweet Green Pea Soup

This is an elegant light soup that is perfect as a prelude to dinner. It is good hot or cold. Cooking lettuce with peas is a French technique. It adds flavor and balance to the peas and is a good way to use up lettuce that is about to pass its peak. However, this soup is quite tasty without that addition. The flavor can easily be varied by using different herbal accents. Mint is the most common, but tarragon, parsley and chives work well, too.

SERVES 6

Start to finish: 20 minutes

EASY EXTRA

✦ For a richer result, stir in ½ cup (125 mL) whipping (35%) cream after the soup has been puréed. Return mixture to saucepan over low heat until heated through.

2 tbsp	butter	25 mL
1 cup	diced onion	250 mL
½ tsp	dried tarragon or thyme leaves	2 mL
½ tsp	salt	2 mL
	Freshly ground black pepper	
10	Boston or romaine lettuce leaves, shredded (optional)	10
4 cups	vegetable or chicken stock	1 L
1	package (12 oz/375 g) frozen sweet green peas	1
Pinch	granulated sugar	Pinch
	Finely chopped parsley or chives	

1. In a large saucepan, melt butter over medium heat. Add onion and cook, stirring, until softened, about 3 minutes. Add tarragon, salt, and black pepper to taste and cook, stirring, for 1 minute. Add lettuce, if using, and stir until wilted.

2. Add chicken stock, green peas and sugar. Bring to a boil. Reduce heat to low and simmer until peas are tender, about 7 minutes.

3. Using a slotted spoon, remove about ¼ cup (50 mL) of the whole peas from the saucepan and set aside. Using a slotted spoon, transfer remaining solids to a food processor or blender. Add ½ cup (125 mL) of the cooking liquid and process until smooth. (You can also do this in the saucepan, using a hand-held blender.) Ladle into bowls and garnish with reserved peas and parsley.

VARIATION: Sweet Green Pea Soup with Mint: Omit tarragon or thyme. Garnish soup with ¼ cup (50 mL) finely chopped mint, along with the whole peas.

Classic Cream of Tomato Soup

This is the soup my mother used to make for special occasions whenever a canned soup wouldn't do. It's delicious and not much more difficult to make than its prepared counterpart.

SERVES 4

Start to finish: 20 minutes

TIP: Purée the soup in the saucepan using a hand-held blender.

EASY EXTRA

✦ Garnish each serving with finely chopped parsley or dill.

1 tbsp	butter	15 mL
1 cup	diced onion	250 mL
Pinch	ground allspice	Pinch
Pinch	cayenne pepper	Pinch
1 tbsp	all-purpose flour	15 mL
2 cups	vegetable or chicken stock	500 mL
1	can (28 oz/796 mL) tomatoes, coarsely chopped, including juice	1
½ cup	whipping (35%) cream	125 mL
	Salt and freshly ground black pepper	

1. In a large saucepan, melt butter over medium heat. Add onion and cook, stirring, until softened, about 3 minutes. Stir in allspice and cayenne. Add flour and cook, stirring, for 1 minute. Add stock and tomatoes with juice. Bring to a boil. Reduce heat to low and simmer for 10 minutes.

2. Using a slotted spoon, transfer solids to a food processor or blender. Add ½ cup (125 mL) of the cooking liquid and process until smooth.

3. Return mixture to saucepan over low heat. Stir in cream and heat through but do not boil. Season with salt and black pepper to taste. Ladle into bowls and serve immediately.

CANNED TOMATOES

Canned tomatoes are one of our most useful convenience foods. In fact, I rarely use anything else, except during the summer when local field tomatoes are in season. The tastiest canned tomatoes come from the San Marzano region of Italy. They are expensive but worth the extra cost. Some North American organically grown tomatoes are also particularly good. Make a point of tasting tomatoes before using them to get a sense of the brands you prefer.

New England Clam Chowder

This classic soup is a meal in itself. I like to serve it with plenty of soda crackers, which is how I ate it when I was a girl.

SERVES 4

Start to finish: 25 minutes

TIP: You can use packaged fully cooked bacon in this recipe. In my experience, precooked bacon strips don't crumble, but you can chop them into small pieces.

2 tbsp	butter	25 mL
1 cup	diced onion	250 mL
1 cup	diced celery	250 mL
3	slices crisp cooked bacon, crumbled, or 3 tbsp (45 mL) precooked real bacon bits (see Tip, left)	3
1 tsp	paprika	5 mL
	Freshly ground black pepper	
2	cans (each 5 oz/142 g) clams, including juice	2
1	can (19 oz/540 mL) whole potatoes, drained and cut into ½-inch (1 cm) cubes, or 2 cups (500 mL) cubed cooked potatoes	1
1	bottle (8 oz/240 mL) clam juice	1
1 cup	water	250 mL
1 cup	whipping (35%) cream	250 mL

1. In a large saucepan, melt butter over medium heat. Add onion and celery and cook, stirring, until softened, about 3 minutes. Add bacon, paprika, and black pepper to taste. Cook, stirring, for 1 minute.

2. Add clams with juice, potatoes, bottled clam juice and water. Bring to a boil. Reduce heat to low and simmer for at least 10 minutes to combine flavors. Stir in cream, remove from heat and serve.

Salads

One of the greatest advances in convenience cooking has been the proliferation of vacuum-sealed bags of washed salad greens. All you add is a flourish or two, such as onion, beets, celery, avocado or palm hearts. Toss with your favorite dressing and enjoy while adding healthful leafy greens to your diet.

There are many excellent bottled salad dressings on the market. However, if you keep it simple, you can quickly make your own (see page 58). For best results, use extra virgin olive oil, not only for taste but also because it is loaded with unsaturated fats, which are good for you. I also recommend keeping a selection of good-quality vinegars on hand as an easy way to add variety to a simple oil and vinegar dressing. These include red and white wine, balsamic, sherry and cider vinegars.

Thai-Style Beef Salad 54

Scandinavian Pasta Salad 55

Carrot, Orange and Onion Salad. 56

Warm Chickpea Salad 58

Tuscan Bean Salad. 59

Mediterranean Potato Salad 60

Chicken Salad Amandine 62

Asian Cucumber Salad 63

Cucumbers in Sour Cream. 63

Beet and Feta Salad. 64

Savory Palm Hearts Salad 66

Palm Hearts Niçoise. 67

ON HAND

- ✓ Extra virgin olive oil
- ✓ A selection of vinegars
- ✓ Mayonnaise
- ✓ Bottled roasted red peppers
- ✓ Preserved anchovies
- ✓ Canned tuna
- ✓ A selection of canned legumes (white kidney beans, chickpeas and lentils)
- ✓ Canned beets and hearts of palm
- ✓ Green or red onion
- ✓ Parsley
- ✓ Bagged washed salad greens that suit your preference

Thai-Style Beef Salad

A more involved version of this recipe is one of my favorite dishes from Andrew Chase's Asian Bistro Cookbook. *I've eaten Andrew's own to-die-for version, made with grilled steak, but rare roast beef from the deli is a delicious alternative. While lime juice is my preference, lemon juice also produces a tasty result. Andrew uses arugula, but bagged mixed salad greens work well, too.*

SERVES 4

Start to finish: 15 minutes

TIPS: In Southeast Asian countries, fish sauce, which is made from brine-covered and fermented fish, is used as widely as soy sauce in China and Japan. It is very pungent but lends an appealing note to many dishes. It is now available in the Asian food section of many supermarkets.

Use bottled preserved lemongrass for convenience. It is available in the Asian sections of many supermarkets and can be stored in the refrigerator after opening.

¼ cup	lime or lemon juice	50 mL
3 tbsp	fish sauce (see Tips, left)	45 mL
2 tsp	minced gingerroot	10 mL
2 tsp	Asian chili sauce (see page 142)	10 mL
4 oz	thinly sliced rare roast beef, chopped, or grilled steak, thinly sliced	125 g
2 cups	diced peeled cucumber	500 mL
1 cup	thinly sliced red or green onions (white part only)	250 mL
4 tbsp	finely chopped cilantro, divided	60 mL
1 tbsp	thinly sliced lemongrass or bottled preserved lemongrass (see Tips, left) or 1 tsp (5 mL) grated lemon zest	15 mL
1	bag (10 oz/300 g) mixed salad greens or 4 cups (1 L) arugula, washed and dried	1
12	cherry tomatoes, halved	12

1. In a bowl, combine lime juice, fish sauce, ginger and chili sauce. Mix well. Add beef, cucumber, onions, 2 tbsp (25 mL) of the cilantro and lemongrass. Toss to combine.

2. Spread salad greens over a deep platter or serving plate. Arrange meat mixture on top. Surround with cherry tomatoes and garnish with remaining cilantro. Serve immediately.

MAXIMIZE CONVENIENCE BY USING:

✦ Bottled or frozen lemon juice
✦ Bottled minced gingerroot
✦ Deli roast beef
✦ Bottled lemongrass
✦ Bagged washed salad greens

Scandinavian Pasta Salad

This salad is so tasty yet so easy to make that it has been a staple at our house for many years. It is also a great dish to contribute to a potluck buffet. I like to use tricolored pasta, which adds visual interest and creates the impression of effort, but the salad tastes just as delicious made with plain macaroni.

SERVES 4

Start to finish: 15 minutes
Chilling: 2 hours

TIPS: If you can't find rotini, use macaroni instead.

Shredded Black Forest ham is usually available at the deli counter. It is so thinly sliced that the pieces are not whole. To ensure that the ham is evenly distributed throughout the salad, you may want to chop the shreds into smaller bits. If you don't see shredded ham, many delis will shred it for you upon request.

EASY EXTRA

✦ Add 2 tbsp (25 mL) finely chopped dill or parsley to mayonnaise mixture before blending.

2 cups	rotini or fusilli pasta, preferably tricolor	500 mL
½ cup	mayonnaise	125 mL
½ cup	sour cream	125 mL
1 tbsp	Dijon mustard	15 mL
½ tsp	salt	2 mL
	Freshly ground black pepper	
8 oz	shredded smoked deli ham, such as Black Forest ham or diced cooked ham (see Tips, left)	250 g
1	roasted red pepper, diced	1
2	hard-cooked eggs, thinly sliced	2
	Dill or parsley sprigs for garnish (optional)	

1. In a pot of boiling salted water, cook pasta until tender to the bite, about 8 minutes. Drain and rinse under cold running water.

2. In a serving bowl, mix together mayonnaise, sour cream, Dijon mustard, salt, and black pepper to taste. Add cooked pasta, ham and roasted red pepper. Toss to combine. Chill thoroughly. Garnish with sliced egg, and dill, if using, just before serving.

HARD-COOKED EGGS

Hard-cooked eggs, sliced or quartered, are an easy way to add nutrients, substance and variety to salads. They can also make an attractive garnish. I prefer to use the cold-water cooking method, which is foolproof.

To make hard-cooked eggs: Place eggs in a saucepan and add cold water to cover. Bring to a boil and cook vigorously for 2 minutes. Remove from heat and let stand for 15 minutes. Drain and immediately plunge eggs into a bowl of cold water. Refrigerate until ready to use.

Carrot, Orange and Onion Salad

If your taste buds are tired and looking for a lift, try this delicious and unusual salad.

SERVES 4

Start to finish: 15 minutes

EASY EXTRA

✦ Garnish each serving with finely chopped parsley.

2 cups	peeled sliced carrots, cooked until tender-crisp and plunged into ice water, or 1 can (14 oz/398 mL) carrots, drained	500 mL
1	can (10 oz/284 mL) mandarin orange segments in syrup, drained, syrup reserved	1
½ cup	thinly sliced red onion	125 mL
1 tbsp	lemon juice	15 mL
1 tbsp	orange marmalade	15 mL
1 tbsp	maple syrup or liquid honey	15 mL
	Salt and freshly ground black pepper	

1. In a serving bowl, combine carrots, oranges and onion.

2. In a small bowl, combine lemon juice, marmalade, maple syrup and 2 tbsp (25 mL) reserved syrup from oranges. Mix well. Pour over carrot mixture and toss to combine. Season with salt and black pepper to taste.

ONION

Always have a good supply of onions on hand as they are versatile and add flavor to many dishes. This includes milder onions, such as green onions (scallions) and red onions, which keep well in the refrigerator crisper and can be used raw as a garnish or to flavor uncooked dishes. Stronger globe onions, which have a pungent smell, are invaluable for flavoring cooked dishes and will keep for several weeks in a cool, dark place. Chopped frozen onions are a time-saver and great relief to cooks with sensitive eyes that are likely to water while peeling and chopping strong onions.

Warm Chickpea Salad

This simple salad is delicious and very versatile. It works well as a side salad or on a buffet table. Served with warm crusty bread, it also makes a nice light meal.

SERVES 4

Start to finish: 20 minutes

TIP: To microwave, place chickpeas and chili pepper, if using, in a microwave-safe dish. Microwave, covered, on High, for 5 minutes.

EASY EXTRA

✦ If you like a bit of spice, add 1 dried red chili pepper or ½ tsp (2 mL) hot pepper flakes to the chickpeas when heating. Discard whole chili pepper, if using, before adding dressing. Using hot pepper flakes, which remain in the salad, produces a spicier result.

1	can (19 oz/540 mL) chickpeas, including liquid	1
½ cup	bottled oil and vinegar dressing or Vinaigrette (see recipe, below)	125 mL
½ cup	finely chopped parsley	125 mL
¼ cup	chopped pitted black olives	50 mL
2 tbsp	prepared basil pesto sauce	25 mL

1. In a saucepan over medium heat, bring chickpeas with liquid to a boil. Simmer for 2 minutes. (You can also do this in a microwave; see Tip, left.) Drain in a colander and rinse well in warm water.

2. Transfer mixture to a serving bowl. Add dressing, parsley, olives and pesto sauce. Toss well.

VINAIGRETTE

The French word for an oil and vinegar dressing seasoned with salt and pepper is vinaigrette. It is the most basic salad dressing and is very easy to make. The quality and taste can be varied dramatically, depending upon the ingredients used. Extra virgin olive oil is my first choice, not only for its taste but because it is a healthful monounsaturated fat. White wine, red wine, balsamic and sherry vinegars all produce delightfully delicious results, as does lemon juice. The basic blend can be enhanced with the addition of such ingredients as mustard, herbs, shallots and garlic. Here's a simple recipe that can be used instead of bottled oil and vinegar dressing in any of the recipes in this book.

Vinaigrette (Oil and Vinegar Dressing): In a large measuring cup with a pouring spout, combine ¼ cup (50 mL) red wine vinegar, 1 tsp (5 mL) salt and ½ tsp (2 mL) black pepper, or to taste. Stir well to dissolve salt. Gradually whisk in ¾ cup (175 mL) extra virgin olive oil until blended. Pour into a bottle, close tightly and refrigerate for up to 1 week. Bring to room temperature if oil has solidified. Shake well before using. Makes 1 cup (250 mL).

Tuscan Bean Salad

Succulent white beans, prepared in a variety of ways, are a staple in Tuscany, Italy. Combined with tuna and a robust vinaigrette, they make a delectable salad. Served with hot crusty bread, this salad is a meal in itself. It also does double duty as a buffet table dish, and when kept chilled, it is a great addition to a picnic basket. If you prefer, use this mixture as a topping for bruschetta (see Variations, right).

SERVES 4

Start to finish: 10 minutes

TIP: If you don't have sun-dried tomato pesto in your refrigerator, use 1 tbsp (15 mL) Dijon mustard or prepared basil pesto instead.

EASY EXTRAS

✦ Half red bell pepper, cored and diced, or finely chopped roasted red pepper, to taste.

✦ Garnish each serving with finely chopped parsley to taste.

1	can (6 oz/170 g) tuna, preferably Italian, packed in olive oil, drained	1
1	can (19 oz/540 mL) white kidney beans, drained and rinsed	1
4	finely chopped green onions (white part only)	4
1 tbsp	prepared sun-dried tomato pesto (see Tip, left)	15 mL
1/2 cup	bottled oil and vinegar dressing or Vinaigrette (see recipe, page 58)	125 mL
	Salt and freshly ground black pepper	

1. In a bowl, combine tuna, beans, green onions and pesto. Pour in oil and vinegar dressing and toss well. Season with salt and black pepper to taste. Serve immediately or refrigerate for at least 2 hours.

VARIATIONS: Salami and White Bean Salad: Substitute 4 oz (125 g) diced salami for the tuna.

Bruschetta with Beans: Lightly brush 6 to 8 slices of country-style bread with olive oil on both sides and toast under the broiler, turning once. Spoon the bean salad evenly over the bread and serve.

CANNED TUNA

Always have a good supply of canned tuna in your pantry as it is a tasty and versatile ingredient. For best results, use Italian tuna packed in olive oil; it is more moist and flavorful than the paler versions packed in water.

Mediterranean Potato Salad

Here's a variation of salade Niçoise, a famous Provençal dish that has long been one of my favorite light meals. Use this recipe to make a minimalist version using tuna, potatoes, chopped onion and capers, then add whatever Easy Extras you have on hand.

SERVES 4

Start to finish: 15 minutes

TIP: If you prefer a more robust dressing, try this herb-flavored vinaigrette. It's very easy to make using a mini food chopper.
Herb-Flavored Vinaigrette: In a bowl, combine 1 finely chopped shallot, 2 tbsp (25 mL) minced parsley or chives, 2 tbsp (25 mL) white wine vinegar and 1 tbsp (15 mL) Dijon mustard. Mix well. Whisk in $1/2$ cup (125 mL) extra virgin olive oil until blended.

EASY EXTRAS

✦ Finely chopped red or green bell pepper

✦ Chopped bottled roasted red pepper

✦ Green beans

✦ Marinated artichoke hearts, quartered

✦ Black olives, pitted and chopped

1	can (6 oz/170 g) tuna, preferably Italian, packed in olive oil, drained	1
1	can (19 oz/540 mL) sliced new potatoes, drained, or 2 cups (500 mL) sliced cooked potatoes	500 mL
¼ cup	chopped green onion	50 mL
1 tbsp	drained capers	15 mL
¾ cup	bottled oil and vinegar dressing or Vinaigrette (see recipe, page 58)	175 mL
1	bag (10 oz/300 g) washed salad greens or 4 cups (1 L) torn lettuce, washed and dried	1
2	hard-cooked eggs (see page 55), quartered or thinly sliced (optional)	2

1. In a bowl, combine tuna, potatoes, onion and capers. Add dressing and toss to combine.

2. Arrange salad greens in a shallow serving dish or deep platter. Spoon tuna mixture over top. Garnish with sliced egg, if using.

MAXIMIZE CONVENIENCE
BY USING:

✦ Canned sliced potatoes, drained

✦ Bottled oil and vinegar dressing

✦ Bagged washed salad greens

Chicken Salad Amandine

This old-fashioned recipe is a great way to use up leftover chicken. It makes a delicious luncheon dish or a light one-course dinner. The quantity of dressing may seem substantial for the amount of chicken, but it also dresses the salad greens.

SERVES 4

Start to finish: 20 minutes

TIP: *To toast almonds:* In a dry nonstick skillet over medium heat, stir almonds constantly until golden brown, 3 to 4 minutes. Immediately transfer to a small bowl to prevent burning.

EASY EXTRAS

✦ Marinated artichoke hearts, quartered

✦ Chopped water chestnuts

¼ cup	mayonnaise	50 mL
2 tbsp	olive oil	25 mL
2 tbsp	lemon juice	25 mL
½ tsp	salt	2 mL
	Freshly ground black pepper	
4 cups	cubed (½ inch/1 cm) cooked chicken	1 L
½ cup	finely chopped celery	125 mL
2 tbsp	finely chopped red or green onion	25 mL
1	bag (10 oz/300 g) washed salad greens, such as hearts of romaine, or 4 cups (1 L) torn lettuce, washed and dried	1
2 tbsp	toasted slivered or sliced almonds (see Tip, left)	25 mL

1. In a bowl, combine mayonnaise, olive oil, lemon juice, salt, and black pepper to taste.

2. In a separate bowl, combine chicken, celery and onion. Add mayonnaise mixture. Toss to combine.

3. Spread salad greens over a deep platter. Spoon chicken mixture on top. Garnish with almonds and serve immediately.

VARIATION: Chicken Salad Sandwich: Omit the salad greens and almonds and use the chicken mixture as a filling for sandwiches. Add sliced tomato, lettuce and/or cucumber slices, as desired.

Asian Cucumber Salad

This simple salad makes a delicious addition to any meal.

SERVES 2

Start to finish: 5 minutes

TIP: Made from fermented rice, this Asian vinegar, which is milder than traditional North American vinegars, is now widely available in supermarkets. Keep a bottle on hand to add its unique flavor to Asian-inspired dishes.

2 tbsp	rice vinegar (see Tip, left)	25 mL
1 tbsp	soy sauce	15 mL
1 tbsp	vegetable oil	15 mL
1	cucumber, peeled and sliced	1
	Salt and freshly ground black pepper	

1. In a serving bowl, combine vinegar, soy sauce and oil. Add cucumber and toss to combine. Season with salt and black pepper to taste. Serve.

Cucumbers in Sour Cream

When I was a teenager, this salad was a specialty at the home of one of my best friends, and it has remained a favorite ever since. This combination is particularly good when cucumbers are in season and at their peak of sweetness.

SERVES 2

Start to finish: 5 minutes

1	cucumber, peeled and sliced	1
1/4 cup	sour cream	50 mL
	Salt and freshly ground black pepper	
	Finely chopped dill (optional)	

1. In a serving bowl, combine cucumber and sour cream. Toss well. Season with salt and black pepper to taste. Garnish with dill, if using.

CUCUMBERS

Learn to think of the cucumber as a convenience food that doesn't come out of a package or a jar. This crunchy vegetable can instantly be transformed into a delicious salad with virtually no work (just slice and toss with sour cream, as I've done above, or oil and vinegar dressing). It is also a great crudité, complementing many spread and dips. Stored in a perforated vegetable bag in the crisper, cucumbers will easily keep for a week.

Beet and Feta Salad

I particularly like the combination of beets and feta cheese in this tasty salad.

SERVES 4

Start to finish: 10 minutes
Chilling: 1 hour

TIPS: If you don't have time to chill the beet mixture, keep the canned beets refrigerated so they will be cold when you're ready to use them.

If using whole baby beets, halve before using.

EASY EXTRA

✦ Add 1 tsp (5 mL) lemon juice with the dressing in Step 1.

1	can (14 oz/398 mL) sliced beets or whole baby beets, drained	1
½ cup	finely chopped celery	125 mL
¼ cup	bottled oil and vinegar dressing or Vinaigrette (see recipe, page 58)	50 mL
½	bag (10 oz/300 g) washed salad greens or 2 cups (500 mL) torn lettuce, washed and dried	½
2 oz	crumbled feta cheese	60 g

1. In a salad bowl, combine beets, celery and dressing. Cover and refrigerate for at least 1 hour or overnight.

2. Add salad greens and toss well. Sprinkle feta over top and serve immediately.

VARIATIONS: Beet and Avocado Salad: Substitute ¼ cup (50 mL) finely chopped green onion for the celery and 1 avocado, cut into ½-inch (1 cm) cubes, for the feta. Cut avocado and add to greens just before tossing.

Beet and Celery Salad: Omit the feta and salad greens and increase the celery to 2 cups (500 mL) sliced. Combine beets and celery in a rectangular dish or on a platter. Mix 1 tsp (5 mL) lemon juice into the dressing and pour the mixture over the vegetables. Or, for a change, try this dressing: Mix 2 tbsp (25 mL) oil and vinegar dressing with 2 tbsp (25 mL) mayonnaise. If desired, add 1 tsp (5 mL) horseradish.

BEETS

Although beets are traditionally served hot as a vegetable side dish, cold sliced or diced beets are a delicious and colorful addition to plain green salads. In markets in France, cooked fresh beets are widely available for this purpose, but in North America, canned beets are the convenient solution. They combine well with a variety of salad dressings, from mayonnaise to simple vinaigrette.

Savory Palm Hearts Salad

This elegant salade composé is substantial enough to serve as a main course. Just add crusty rolls.

SERVES 4	

Start to finish: 15 minutes

TIP: You can easily turn this into a main course salad by adding ingredients such as thinly sliced ham, sliced red bell pepper and sliced tomatoes. Treat them as a substantial garnish and arrange them attractively around the palm hearts. Depending upon the quantity you add, you may want to double the red pepper sauce. Save any leftover sauce to use as a dip.

EASY EXTRAS

✦ Shredded ham, torn into bite-size pieces

✦ Slivers red bell pepper

✦ Sliced tomatoes (in season) or cherry tomatoes, halved

RED PEPPER SAUCE

1	roasted red pepper, chopped	1
2	slices Black Forest ham, coarsely chopped	2
¼ cup	mayonnaise	50 mL
2 tsp	lemon juice	10 mL
¼ tsp	salt	1 mL
	Freshly ground black pepper	
1	can (14 oz/398 mL) hearts of palm, drained and rinsed	1
1	bag (10 oz/300 g) hearts of romaine, torn, or 4 cups (1 L) torn lettuce, washed and dried	1

1. *Red Pepper Sauce:* In a food processor, combine roasted pepper, chopped ham, mayonnaise, lemon juice, salt, and black pepper to taste. Process until smooth.

2. Cut palm hearts in half lengthwise. Spread romaine hearts evenly over a deep platter. Arrange cut palm hearts, curved side up, in a row down the middle. Spoon red pepper sauce evenly over palm hearts. Serve immediately.

VARIATION: Ham and Red Pepper Dip: To turn this recipe into an appetizer, omit the salad greens and double the quantity of the red pepper sauce. Use 2 cans hearts of palm. Spoon the sauce into a small bowl. Arrange the cut palm hearts on a small oval platter or a serving plate. Pass napkins and dip the palm hearts into the sauce.

Palm Hearts Niçoise

This tasty and nutritious salad, which is substantial enough to serve four as a main course, has a Provençal feel. It's ideal for lunch and makes a great dinner for those evenings when you're tired of the same old thing.

SERVES 6

Start to finish: 15 minutes
Chilling: 1 hour

TIP: Cut the avocado just before serving; otherwise it will turn brown.

1	can (14 oz/398 mL) hearts of palm, drained and rinsed	1
1/4 cup	bottled oil and vinegar dressing or Vinaigrette (see recipe, page 58)	50 mL
2 tbsp	finely chopped parsley	25 mL
2 tbsp	drained capers	25 mL
1	bag (10 oz/300 g) washed salad greens or 4 cups (1 L) torn lettuce, washed and dried	1
1	avocado, cut into 1/4-inch (0.5 cm) wedges (see Tip, left)	1
2	hard-cooked eggs (see page 55), peeled and cut into quarters	2

1. Cut hearts of palm into 1/2-inch (1 cm) slices.
2. In a bowl, combine palm hearts, dressing, parsley and capers. Toss to combine. Refrigerate for at least 1 hour or overnight.
3. Arrange salad greens over a deep platter. Top with chilled palm heart mixture, sliced avocado and eggs. Serve immediately.

HEARTS OF PALM

Canned hearts of palm, which resemble white asparagus without the tips, make a smart addition to any pantry. This delicious food is the inner stem of a type of palm tree. Thick and round, it has a firm chewy texture and a delicate flavor, not unlike asparagus. It can be tossed with oil and vinegar dressing and served as a salad on its own, or cut into 1-inch (2.5 cm) lengths and added to tossed salads. It can also be served as an appetizer with a mayonnaise-based dip (see Ham and Red Pepper Dip variation, page 66). Before using canned hearts of palm, drain and rinse under cold running water, then soak in 1 tbsp (15 mL) lemon juice and water to cover for 10 minutes. Drain before using in any recipe.

Eggs and Meatless Mains

The recipes in this chapter are intended to meet the needs of health-conscious consumers who are trying to reduce their consumption of meat. Relying for the most part on tasty combinations of cheese, legumes, eggs and an assortment of vegetables, these dishes are nutritious and satisfying. As one of nature's own convenience foods, eggs are the focal point. They cook quickly and are delicious simply prepared. With the addition of a few ingredients, they can easily be transformed into a special meal. Furthermore, eggs are an excellent source of protein and are rich in many vitamins and minerals.

Egg Foo Yung with Chinese Vegetables 70

Spinach Frittata 71

Italian-Style Poached Eggs 72

Cheese and Hash Brown Omelet 74

Best-Ever Scrambled Eggs 75

Eggs Rancheros with Black Bean Sauce 76

Simple Succotash 77

Zesty Black Bean Pie 78

Enchiladas in Salsa Verde 80

Lentil Shepherd's Pie 81

Tomato Gratin 82

Falafel in Pita 84

Spinach Risotto 85

Very Veggie Chili 86

ON HAND

✓ Fresh eggs

✓ Prepared pesto sauce (sun-dried tomato and basil)

✓ Frozen spinach

✓ Chinese vegetables for stir-fry

✓ Canned tomatoes, corn and potatoes

✓ A selection of canned legumes (black beans, lentils and red kidney beans)

Egg Foo Yung with Chinese Vegetables

I've always been fond of egg foo yung, a dish that seems to have fallen off the radar screens in Chinese restaurants as more sophisticated fare has gained popularity. In addition to being very tasty, this variation adds a healthy serving of vegetables to your diet. Don't worry about leftovers: like a good Spanish omelet (tortilla), this dish is also good cold.

SERVES 4

Prep: 10 minutes
Baking: 15 minutes

+ PREHEAT OVEN TO 350°F (180°C)
+ OVENPROOF SKILLET WITH HEATPROOF HANDLE (SEE TIP, PAGE 71)

6	eggs, beaten	6
3 tbsp	finely chopped green onions	45 mL
1/4 tsp	salt	1 mL
	Freshly ground black pepper	
1 tbsp	vegetable oil	15 mL
2 cups	frozen mixed Chinese vegetables for stir-fry	500 mL
2 tbsp	soy sauce	25 mL

1. In a bowl, whisk together eggs, green onions, salt, and black pepper to taste. Set aside.

2. In an ovenproof skillet, heat oil over medium heat. Add vegetables and stir-fry until tender, about 6 minutes. Stir in soy sauce.

3. Pour egg mixture over vegetables. Bake in preheated oven until egg is firmly set, about 15 minutes. Cut into wedges and serve.

VARIATIONS: Crab Foo Yung with Chinese Vegetables: Stir in 1 can (4 oz/125 g) crab, drained, along with the soy sauce.

Shrimp Foo Yung with Chinese Vegetables: Stir in 1 can (3¾ oz/106 g) shrimp, drained, or ½ cup (125 mL) cooked salad shrimp along with the soy sauce.

Spinach Frittata

A frittata is an Italian omelet in which the ingredients are cooked with the eggs rather than being folded into them, French style. There are several methods for making this versatile dish. I prefer this one — which partially cooks the eggs on top of the stove, then finishes them in the oven — as it is essentially foolproof.

SERVES 2

Start to finish: 20 minutes

TIP: If the handle of your skillet is not ovenproof, wrap it in aluminum foil.

✦ PREHEAT OVEN TO 425°F (220°C)
✦ OVENPROOF SKILLET WITH HEATPROOF HANDLE AND LID (SEE TIP, LEFT)

6	eggs, beaten	6
1 tbsp	vegetable oil	15 mL
½ cup	diced onion	125 mL
1 tsp	dried Italian seasoning	5 mL
½ tsp	salt	2 mL
	Freshly ground black pepper	
1	package (10 oz/300 g) frozen chopped spinach, thawed and squeezed dry, or 1 package (10 oz/300 g) spinach, washed, stems removed and chopped	1
¼ cup	grated Parmesan cheese	50 mL
2 tbsp	prepared sun-dried tomato pesto	25 mL

1. In a bowl, lightly beat eggs. Set aside.

2. In an ovenproof skillet, heat oil over medium heat. Add onion and cook, stirring, until softened, about 3 minutes. Stir in Italian seasoning, salt, and black pepper to taste. Add spinach and stir well.

3. Reduce heat to low. Cover and cook until spinach is wilted, about 5 minutes. Slowly pour eggs over spinach. Increase heat to medium. Cover and cook until mixture begins to form a crust on the bottom, 2 to 3 minutes.

4. Sprinkle with Parmesan cheese and transfer pan to preheated oven. Bake, uncovered, until eggs are set but frittata is still soft in the center, about 3 minutes. Cut into wedges and serve topped with a dollop of pesto.

Italian-Style Poached Eggs

For those times when plain poached eggs just won't do, here's an Italian-inspired version that is flavorful and delightfully different. I enjoy this as a light dinner, but it also makes an outstanding dish for brunch.

SERVES 2

Start to finish: 10 minutes

TIP: If you don't have a can of seasoned tomatoes on hand, here's how to make your own. In a small skillet, heat 1 tbsp (15 mL) olive oil over medium heat. Add 2 tbsp (25 mL) diced onion and cook, stirring, until softened, about 3 minutes. Stir in 1 tsp (5 mL) minced garlic and 1/2 tsp (2 mL) dried Italian seasoning. Coarsely chop 2 cups (500 mL) tomatoes or use 1 can (19 oz/540 mL) tomatoes with juice, and add to pan. Bring to a boil. Taste and adjust seasoning. Reduce heat to low and proceed with Step 2.

1	**can (19 oz/540 mL) chunky tomatoes with roasted garlic and basil (see Tip, left)**	1
	Salt and freshly ground black pepper	
4	**eggs**	4
2	**slices country-style bread, toasted**	2

1. In a small skillet over medium heat, bring tomatoes to a boil. Taste and season with salt and black pepper. Reduce heat to low.

2. Break eggs into pan. Cover and cook until whites are set and yolks are still soft, 3 to 4 minutes. Serve over toasted bread.

VARIATION: Baked Eggs with Parmesan: If you prefer a cheesier version of this dish, preheat the broiler and heat the tomatoes in an ovenproof skillet with a heatproof handle. When the eggs are almost set, sprinkle them with 2 tbsp (25 mL) grated Parmesan cheese. Place the pan under the broiler for a minute until the cheese is melted and brown.

POACHED EGGS

In my opinion, a perfectly poached egg is a work of art and its enjoyment should not be limited to breakfast. Poached eggs are wonderful for brunch and lunch and also make a great light dinner dish. To make a visually perfect poached egg, buy egg-poaching rings at a kitchen store or use the rings from canning jars.

To poach eggs: In a saucepan, bring about 2 inches (5 cm) lightly salted water to a boil over medium heat. Reduce heat to low and drop poaching rings into water. Break eggs, one at a time, into a measuring cup and pour one egg into each ring. Or holding the cup close to the surface of the water, slip the egg into the saucepan; repeat with remaining eggs. Cook until whites are set and centers are still soft, 3 to 4 minutes. Remove from water using a slotted spoon.

Cheese and Hash Brown Omelet

Here's a hearty, no-nonsense dish that is a particular favorite with teenagers, although adults enjoy it, too. It's very easy to make, and with preshredded cheese, it can be completed from start to finish in less than 15 minutes. Add a crisp green salad and crusty rolls for a great-tasting meal.

SERVES 2

Start to finish: 15 minutes

TIP: I prefer this omelet to be a bit soft in the middle. If you prefer a firmer result, leave it in the oven for a little longer.

EASY EXTRAS

+ For a spicier omelet, add hot pepper sauce, to taste, when beating the eggs.
+ Add 1/2 tsp (2 mL) paprika along with the black pepper when seasoning the potatoes.

+ PREHEAT OVEN TO 425°F (220°C)
+ OVENPROOF SKILLET WITH HEATPROOF HANDLE (SEE TIP, PAGE 71)

6	**eggs**	6
1/4 tsp	**salt**	1 mL
2 tbsp	**vegetable oil, divided**	25 mL
1 cup	**frozen hash brown potatoes**	250 mL
	Freshly ground black pepper	
1 cup	**shredded Cheddar or Swiss cheese**	250 mL

1. In a bowl, lightly beat eggs and salt. Set aside.

2. In an ovenproof skillet, heat 1 tbsp (15 mL) of the oil over medium heat. Add potatoes and season with black pepper to taste. Cook, stirring, until potatoes are crisp and browned, 7 to 8 minutes. Transfer to a paper towel-lined plate to drain and wipe skillet clean.

3. Add remaining oil to skillet and return to heat. Add egg mixture and cook until mixture begins to form a crust on the bottom, about 2 minutes.

4. Sprinkle cheese evenly over top and arrange potatoes evenly over cheese. Bake in preheated oven until eggs are set and cheese is melted, 2 to 3 minutes.

KNOW YOUR EGGS

The best eggs are free-range and organic. Not only do they taste better, they are less likely to be infected with disease than eggs that are produced in crowded conditions. Although all eggs should be used prior to the "best before" date on the carton, eggs lose flavor along with freshness. Use newer eggs for eating and save older ones for baking. You can tell if an egg is fresh by dropping it in a bowl of water. A fresh egg will sink, but an older egg will float.

Best-Ever Scrambled Eggs

When I'm on my own, scrambled eggs are one of my favorite dinners. I like them plain, accompanied by whole grain toast, or with smoked salmon or even a little pesto sauce (see Variations, right). I credit my Irish-born grandmother for teaching me to make them with cream, although lower-fat milk will do if you're watching your fat intake. For a traditional breakfast, add ham, sausage or crisp bacon and lots of hot buttered toast. Double or triple this recipe as required.

SERVES 2

Start to finish: 10 minutes

EASY EXTRA

✦ For a little bit of spice, add a pinch of cayenne pepper with the salt and pepper.

4	eggs	4
¼ cup	cream or milk	50 mL
¼ tsp	salt	1 mL
	Freshly ground black pepper	
1 tbsp	butter	15 mL

1. In a bowl, whisk together eggs, cream, salt, and black pepper to taste. Set aside.

2. In a saucepan, melt butter over low heat. Add egg mixture and cook just until eggs begin to set, about 2 minutes. Begin to stir, scraping up set bits from the bottom, and stir constantly until the mixture is setting but still moist, about 3 minutes. Remove from heat and serve immediately.

VARIATIONS: Scrambled Eggs with Smoked Salmon: Accompany eggs with 2 slices smoked salmon per serving and garnish with 1 tbsp (15 mL) finely chopped green onion or chives.

Mexican-Style Scrambled Eggs: Add 1 tsp (5 mL) finely chopped jalapeño pepper (alternatively, add hot pepper sauce to beaten eggs, to taste), ¼ cup (50 mL) cooked or thawed corn kernels and ¼ cup (50 mL) diced cured chorizo sausage to saucepan along with the butter. Stir in 2 tbsp (25 mL) salsa after the eggs are cooked. Be sure to use cured cooked chorizo sausage (which is hard) as the uncooked variety will not cook in this recipe. Serve with sliced tomatoes in season.

Scrambled Eggs with Pesto: Just before serving, stir 1 to 2 tbsp (15 to 25 mL) basil pesto into the eggs.

Scrambled Eggs with Fine Herbs: Sprinkle cooked eggs with any combination of the following mixture of fresh herbs, to taste: finely chopped parsley, chives, basil, tarragon, marjoram and thyme.

Eggs Rancheros with Black Bean Sauce

Here is an absolutely delicious and nutritious dinner. Add the Avocado Salad (see Tips, below) for a special treat and nutritional boost. This quantity serves four, but the amounts can easily be reduced. Use two tortillas and two eggs per person. Use leftover bean sauce as a dip for tortilla chips. Just reheat until it is hot and bubbling.

SERVES 4

Start to finish: 15 minutes

TIPS: *Avocado Salad:* In a bowl, combine 2 tbsp (25 mL) each finely chopped green onion and cilantro. Add 1 tbsp (15 mL) lime juice and 1 avocado, chopped into ½-inch (1 cm) cubes. Toss to combine.

To toast cumin seeds: Before making the black bean sauce, heat the seeds in a dry skillet over medium heat, stirring, until they release their aroma and just begin to brown, about 2 minutes. Immediately transfer to a mortar or a cutting board. With a pestle or a rolling pin or can, crush the seeds to the desired consistency.

1 tbsp	vegetable oil	15 mL
½ cup	diced onion	125 mL
1 tsp	minced garlic	5 mL
1 tsp	cumin seeds, toasted and ground (see Tips, left), or ½ tsp (2 mL) ground cumin	5 mL
½ tsp	salt	2 mL
¼ tsp	freshly ground black pepper	1 mL
1	can (19 oz/540 mL) black beans, drained and rinsed	1
½ cup	tomato salsa	125 mL
1 cup	shredded Monterey Jack cheese	250 mL
8	tortillas, warmed	8
8	eggs, poached (see page 72)	8

1. In a skillet, heat oil over medium heat. Add onion and cook, stirring, until softened, about 3 minutes. Add garlic, cumin seeds, salt and black pepper and cook, stirring, for 1 minute. Add beans and salsa and bring to a boil. Add cheese and stir until melted, about 1 minute. Place 4 tortillas on serving plates and spread with bean mixture.

2. Place 2 poached eggs on each bean-topped tortilla. Serve the other tortilla on the side.

MAXIMIZE CONVENIENCE
BY USING:
- Frozen diced onion
- Bottled or frozen minced garlic
- Already shredded cheese

Simple Succotash

Succotash is a traditional American dish, apparently of Native origin. Although there are many versions, it almost always contains corn and lima beans, and in pioneer times was made with salt pork. Here's a quick and meatless version. Fish lovers may want to accompany this recipe with a simple breaded fillet (try the Parmesan-Crusted Snapper on page 91 and hold the sauce) as the combination is delicious. Add the cream (see Easy Extras, below) if you prefer a creamy sauce.

SERVES 4

Start to finish: 25 minutes

EASY EXTRAS

✦ Add 1 chopped red or green bell pepper or frozen mixed bell pepper strips along with the garlic, or stir in 1 chopped roasted red pepper along with the corn.

✦ If you prefer a creamy sauce, stir in ¹/₂ cup (125 mL) whipping (35%) cream just before serving.

1 tbsp	vegetable oil	15 mL
1 cup	diced onion	250 mL
1 tbsp	minced garlic	15 mL
¹/₂ tsp	dried Italian seasoning	2 mL
	Salt and freshly ground black pepper	
2 cups	tomato sauce	500 mL
2	cans (each 12 oz/375 g) corn kernels, drained, or 1¹/₂ cups (375 mL) frozen corn kernels, thawed	2
2	cans (each 14 oz/398 mL) baby lima beans, drained and rinsed	2

1. In a skillet, heat oil over medium heat. Add onion and cook, stirring, until softened, about 3 minutes. Add garlic, Italian seasoning and salt and black pepper to taste, and cook, stirring, for 1 minute.

2. Stir in tomato sauce, corn and lima beans. Bring to a boil. Reduce heat to low and simmer until vegetables are tender, about 15 minutes.

MAXIMIZE CONVENIENCE BY USING:

✦ Frozen diced onion
✦ Bottled or frozen minced garlic
✦ Prepared tomato sauce

Zesty Black Bean Pie

If your taste buds have grown weary of the old standards, try this savory pie with a cracker crumb crust. Just add a simple green salad for a nutritious and tasty meal.

SERVES 4

Prep: 20 minutes
Baking: 10 minutes

TIPS: Use a mild or hot tomato salsa, depending upon your preference.

You can also use a blender to make the cracker crumbs. Add the crackers in batches and process, scraping down the sides after each addition.

EASY EXTRAS

✦ Add 1 jalapeño pepper, finally chopped, along with the garlic.

✦ Add 1 or 2 finely chopped roasted red peppers along with the corn.

✦ PREHEAT OVEN TO 350°F (180°C)
✦ 9-INCH (23 CM) PIE PLATE

CRUST

30	cheese-flavored crackers, such as Ritz (about half an 8-oz/250 g box)	30
¼ cup	butter, melted	50 mL

FILLING

1 tbsp	vegetable oil	15 mL
1 cup	diced onion	250 mL
1 tsp	minced garlic	5 mL
1 tsp	ground cumin	5 mL
1	can (19 oz/540 mL) black beans, drained and rinsed	1
1	can (12 oz/341 mL) corn kernels, drained	1
1 cup	tomato salsa	250 mL
4 oz	cream cheese, cut into ½-inch (1 cm) cubes and softened	125 g

1. *Crust:* In a food processor or blender (see Tips, left), pulse crackers until they resemble coarse crumbs.

2. In a bowl, combine cracker crumbs and butter. Press into pie plate. Bake in preheated oven until golden, about 8 minutes.

3. *Filling:* Meanwhile, in a skillet, heat oil over medium heat. Add onion and cook, stirring, until softened, about 3 minutes. Add garlic and cumin and cook, stirring, for 1 minute.

4. Stir in beans, corn and salsa. Bring to a boil. Add cream cheese, and cook, stirring, until cheese is melted and mixture holds together, about 2 minutes. Remove from heat.

5. Spread mixture evenly over cooked crust. Bake in preheated oven for 10 minutes to combine flavors.

Enchiladas in Salsa Verde

This tasty variation of a classic Mexican dish has an appealing combination of ingredients and flavors. Serve with a simple avocado and onion salad for a meal with a south-of-the-border theme.

SERVES 4 TO 6

Prep: 5 minutes
Baking: 30 minutes

TIPS: Salsa verde is available in the Mexican foods section of many supermarkets or in specialty food stores.

Corn tortillas have a more authentic Mexican flavor than those made with flour, and I like to use them in Mexican-inspired dishes. In some locales they can be difficult to find, so I often buy several packages and freeze them. They take an hour or so to thaw at room temperature, but you can speed up the process in the microwave.

EASY EXTRAS

✦ If you are a heat seeker, add 1 finely chopped jalapeño pepper along with the garlic.

✦ Add garnishes such as finely chopped red or green onion, finely chopped coriander, shredded lettuce or sour cream.

✦ PREHEAT OVEN TO 350°F (180°C)
✦ 13-BY 9-INCH (3 L) BAKING DISH

1 tbsp	vegetable oil	15 mL
1 cup	diced onion	250 mL
1 tbsp	minced garlic	15 mL
1 tsp	ground cumin	5 mL
1	can (19 oz/540 mL) whole potatoes, drained and diced, or 2 cups (500 mL) diced cooked potatoes	1
1	package (10 oz/300 g) frozen chopped spinach, including liquid, thawed, or 1 bag (10 oz/300 g) spinach, stems removed and coarsely chopped	1
1	can (14 oz/398 mL) refried beans	1
3 cups	shredded Monterey Jack cheese or Mexican cheese mix, divided	750 mL
3 cups	salsa verde, divided (see Tips, left)	750 mL
16	6-inch (15 cm) tortillas, preferably corn (see Tips, left)	16

1. In a skillet, heat oil over medium heat. Add onion and cook, stirring, until softened, about 3 minutes. Add garlic and cumin and cook, stirring, for 1 minute. Add potatoes and spinach and cook, stirring, until spinach is incorporated, about 3 minutes. Stir in refried beans and bring to a boil. Add $1\frac{3}{4}$ cups (425 mL) of the cheese and cook, stirring, until cheese melts, about 2 minutes. Remove from heat.

2. Pour 1 cup (250 mL) of the salsa verde into a bowl. One at a time, dip tortillas into sauce, turning to ensure all parts are moistened. Lay 1 tortilla on a plate and spread with a generous $\frac{1}{4}$ cup (50 mL) of the bean mixture. Roll up and place, seam side down, in baking dish. Repeat with remaining tortillas until all the filling is used.

3. Pour remaining salsa verde over tortillas and sprinkle with remaining cheese. Cover and bake in preheated oven until hot and bubbling, about 30 minutes. Add garnishes (see Easy Extras, left).

Lentil Shepherd's Pie

Here's a flavorful rendition of an old favorite, in which lentils are substituted for the traditional meat. Serve with a tossed salad for a nutritious and satisfying meal.

SERVES 4

Prep: 25 minutes
Baking: 25 minutes

TIPS: Use shredded Cheddar cheese instead of the Italian 4-cheese mixture, if you prefer.

Substitute 1/2 cup (125 mL) loosely packed parsley leaves for the green onions, if you prefer.

Be careful not to overprocess the potato mixture or the topping will be mushy. Small lumps of potato should remain.

✦ PREHEAT OVEN TO 350°F (180°C)
✦ 8-CUP (2 L) BAKING DISH, LIGHTLY GREASED

TOPPING

1	can (19 oz/540 mL) potatoes, drained, or 2 cups (500 mL) cubed cooked potatoes	2
1/2 cup	milk	125 mL
1 cup	shredded Italian 4-cheese mix	250 mL
1/2 cup	dry bread crumbs	125 mL
4	green onions (white part only), coarsely chopped	4
1 tbsp	butter, softened	15 mL
1/2 tsp	salt	2 mL
	Freshly ground black pepper	

FILLING

1 tbsp	vegetable oil	15 mL
2 cups	diced onion	500 mL
1 cup	diced celery	250 mL
1	can (28 oz/796 mL) tomatoes, drained and coarsely chopped	1
1	can (19 oz/540 mL) lentils, drained and rinsed	1
2 tbsp	prepared basil pesto	25 mL
2 tbsp	shredded Italian 4-cheese mix	25 mL

1. *Topping:* In a food processor, combine potatoes and milk. Pulse several times to combine. Add cheese, bread crumbs, onions, butter, salt, and black pepper to taste. Process until blended but potatoes are still a bit lumpy. Set aside.

2. *Filling:* In a skillet, heat oil over medium heat. Add onion and celery and cook, stirring, until celery is softened, about 8 minutes. Add tomatoes and lentils. Bring to a boil. Stir in pesto and pour into prepared baking dish.

3. Spread reserved potato mixture evenly over lentil mixture. Sprinkle with shredded cheese. Bake in preheated oven until top is browned and mixture is bubbling, about 25 minutes.

Tomato Gratin

A gratin is a dish that is topped with cheese or bread crumbs and heated until the top is golden. I make this in a relatively shallow baking dish, which increases the surface area and ensures a good amount of melted cheese per serving. I like to serve this with crusty country-style bread and a Mediterranean-inspired salad. Just open a bag of hearts of romaine, add some chopped green onion and marinated artichoke hearts and toss with oil and vinegar.

SERVES 4

Prep: 15 minutes
Baking: 30 minutes

TIP: Substitute shredded Cheddar cheese for the Italian 4-cheese mix, if desired.

EASY EXTRA

✦ Add 4 chopped anchovies or 4 tsp (20 mL) anchovy paste along with the garlic. If using chopped anchovies, cook the mixture until the anchovies dissolve.

✦ PREHEAT OVEN TO 375°F (190°C)
✦ 6-CUP (1.5 L) SHALLOW BAKING DISH, LIGHTLY GREASED

1 tbsp	vegetable oil	15 mL
2 cups	diced onion	500 mL
1 tbsp	minced garlic	15 mL
1 tsp	dried Italian seasoning	5 mL
1 tsp	salt	5 mL
	Freshly ground black pepper	
1	can (28 oz/796 mL) tomatoes, drained and coarsely chopped	1
1	can (19 oz/540 mL) sliced potatoes, drained	1
¼ cup	sliced black olives	50 mL
1 cup	shredded Italian 4-cheese mix	250 mL

1. In a skillet, heat oil over medium heat. Add onion and cook, stirring, until softened, about 3 minutes. Add garlic, dried Italian seasoning, salt, and black pepper to taste and cook, stirring, for 1 minute. Add tomatoes and bring to a boil. Reduce heat to low and simmer for 5 minutes.

2. Ladle one-third of the tomato mixture into prepared dish. Arrange potatoes in a single layer over the top. Sprinkle evenly with olives and cover with remaining sauce. Sprinkle cheese evenly over top. Bake in preheated oven until cheese is golden and tomatoes are bubbling and hot, about 30 minutes.

VARIATION: Cauliflower Gratin: Substitute 3 cups (750 mL) blanched cauliflower florets for the potatoes.

Falafel in Pita

These tasty treats are a gift from the Middle East, where they are eaten the way hamburgers are in North America. Liberally garnished, they make a great lunch or light dinner.

SERVES 4

Start to finish: 15 minutes

EASY EXTRA

✦ Add 1 or 2 roasted red peppers to the chickpeas before processing.

1	can (19 oz/540 mL) chickpeas, drained and rinsed	1
½ cup	sliced green onion	125 mL
2 tbsp	lemon juice	25 mL
1 tbsp	minced garlic	15 mL
1 to 2 tsp	curry powder	5 to 10 mL
1	egg	1
2 tbsp	vegetable oil	25 mL
½ cup	all-purpose flour	125 mL
4	pita breads	4
	Chopped peeled cucumber	
	Chopped tomato	
	Shredded lettuce	
	Plain yogurt	

1. In a food processor, combine chickpeas, onion, lemon juice, garlic, and curry powder to taste. Process until blended but chickpeas retain their texture. Using your hands, shape into 4 large patties.

2. In a shallow bowl, lightly beat egg. In a skillet, heat oil over medium heat. Dip each patty into the egg, then into the flour, coating both sides well. Fry until golden and heated through, about 2 minutes per side.

3. Fill each pita bread with a falafel and garnish with cucumber, tomato, lettuce and yogurt, as desired.

MAXIMIZE CONVENIENCE
BY USING:
✦ Bottled or frozen minced garlic
✦ Bottled or frozen lemon juice

Spinach Risotto

Although it needs to bake for 30 minutes, this method for cooking risotto eliminates the tedious task of stirring the liquid until it is absorbed. Add crusty rolls and a crisp green salad for a tasty meal.

SERVES 4

Prep: 15 minutes
Baking: 30 minutes

TIPS: If you don't have a saucepan with an ovenproof handle, transfer the mixture to a deep 6-cup (1.5 L) baking dish after completing Step 1.

To partially thaw the spinach for this recipe, place the package in a microwave and heat on High for 3 minutes. It can easily be separated using a fork but will still have some ice crystals. Do not drain before adding to rice.

EASY EXTRA

✦ Sprinkle 2 tbsp (25 mL) toasted pine nuts over the risotto just before serving. *To toast pine nuts:* Cook, stirring, in a skillet over medium heat. Brown for 3 to 5 minutes. Remove from heat and transfer to a cool bowl.

✦ PREHEAT OVEN TO 400°F (200°C)
✦ OVENPROOF SAUCEPAN WITH HEATPROOF HANDLE (SEE TIPS, LEFT)

2 tbsp	butter	25 mL
1 cup	diced onion	250 mL
1 cup	Arborio rice	250 mL
1 tbsp	minced garlic	15 mL
1	package (10 oz/300 g) frozen spinach, partially thawed (see Tips, left)	1
3 cups	vegetable stock	750 mL
3 tbsp	prepared sun-dried tomato pesto	45 mL
	Grated Parmesan cheese	

1. In an ovenproof saucepan, melt butter over medium heat. Add onion and cook until softened, about 3 minutes. Add rice and cook, stirring, until the grains of rice are coated with butter, about 1 minute. Add spinach and cook, breaking up with a spoon, until thoroughly integrated into the rice, about 2 minutes. Stir in stock and pesto. Bring to a boil.

2. Transfer saucepan to preheated oven and bake, stirring partway through, until rice has absorbed the liquid, about 30 minutes. Remove from oven and sprinkle Parmesan over top. Serve immediately.

MAXIMIZE CONVENIENCE
BY USING:
✦ Frozen diced onion
✦ Bottled or frozen minced garlic
✦ Prepared stock
✦ Prepared pesto sauce

Very Veggie Chili

Here's a tasty vegetarian chili that uses chili powder and tomato sauce spiked with hot peppers to quickly achieve an authentic chili flavor. If made with frozen diced butternut squash (see Variation below), the zucchini chopping is eliminated and the result is even speedier. Serve this the old-fashioned way — with toast — and top with a dollop of sour cream, if desired.

SERVES 4

Start to finish: 25 minutes

1 tbsp	vegetable oil	15 mL
1 cup	diced onion	250 mL
2	medium zucchini, cut into ½-inch (1 cm) cubes (about 1 lb/500 g)	2
1 tbsp	minced garlic	15 mL
1 tbsp	chili powder	15 mL
1	can (12 oz/341 mL) corn kernels, drained, or 1½ cups (375 mL) frozen corn kernels, thawed	1
1	can (19 oz/540 mL) red kidney beans, drained and rinsed	1
2 cups	spicy tomato sauce, such as arrabbiata	500 mL
	Sour cream (optional)	

1. In a skillet, heat oil over medium heat. Add onion and zucchini and cook, stirring occasionally, until zucchini is tender, about 8 minutes. Add garlic and chili powder and cook, stirring, for 1 minute.

2. Add corn, kidney beans and tomato sauce. Bring to a boil. Reduce heat to low and simmer for 10 minutes to combine flavors. Ladle into bowls and top with sour cream, if desired.

VARIATION: Squash and Black Bean Chili: Substitute 3 cups (750 mL) diced butternut squash for the zucchini and 1 can (19 oz/540 mL) black beans for the kidney beans.

MAXIMIZE CONVENIENCE
BY USING:
+ Frozen diced onion
+ Bottled or frozen minced garlic
+ Prepared tomato sauce

Fish and Seafood

In any discussion of convenience foods, canned salmon and tuna would be high on the list of most popular items. While these tasty and versatile foods are indispensable pantry staples, many frozen products, such as fish fillets and shrimp, are just as handy. Not only are these ingredients quick-cooking and loaded with nutrition, they are widely available year-round, making them important contributors to a weekly meal plan. Fish and shrimp can be kept frozen for up to two months. Before using, thaw fish overnight in the refrigerator or on Defrost power in a microwave oven. When using frozen shrimp or smoked salmon, thaw according to package instructions.

Sole, snapper and halibut are firm white-flesh fish. They can be used interchangeably in these recipes, as noted.

Thai-Style Salmon Curry 90

Parmesan-Crusted Snapper
with Tomato Olive Sauce 91

Salmon Burgers 92

Potato Pancakes with Smoked Salmon 94

Salmon Quiche 95

Pan-Fried Halibut in Spicy Lemon Sauce 96

Baked Fish with Tomatoes
and Roasted Red Pepper 98

Paupiettes of Sole Florentine 99

Garlic Chili Shrimp 100

Shrimp in Tomato Sauce with Feta 102

Coconut Shrimp Curry 103

Creamy Corn and Shrimp 104

ON HAND

- ✓ Canned salmon
- ✓ Frozen smoked salmon
- ✓ Bottled roasted red peppers
- ✓ Frozen cooked peeled shrimp
- ✓ Frozen peeled deveined shrimp
- ✓ Frozen firm white fish fillets, such as sole, snapper or halibut
- ✓ Prepared Alfredo sauce
- ✓ Canned coconut milk
- ✓ Green onions

◄ Thai-Style Salmon Curry

Thai-Style Salmon Curry

If, like me, you're fond of Thai food, here's an easy way to taste its unique flavors. Look for fish sauce in the Asian foods section of well-stocked supermarkets.

SERVES 2

Start to finish: 15 minutes

TIPS: This recipe can be doubled or tripled.

Canned or frozen peas work well in this curry. If using canned peas, be sure to drain them before adding to the recipe. Cook frozen peas according to package instructions.

Dried lime leaves (available in Asian markets) can be substituted for the lime juice. Use 4 leaves, torn into thirds, and add along with the chili peppers. Remove along with the chilies.

EASY EXTRAS

✦ Add 1 stick lemongrass, smashed and sliced into 1-inch (2.5 cm) pieces, or 2 pieces of preserved lemongrass along with the chili peppers. Remove along with the chilies.

✦ Garnish with half a red pepper, cut into thin slivers, just before serving.

1	can (14 oz/398 mL) coconut milk	1
1 to 2	fresh chili peppers, minced, or 3 whole dried red chili peppers	1 to 2
1	can (7½ oz/213 g) salmon, drained	1
1 cup	cooked green peas (see Tips, left)	250 mL
2 tbsp	fish sauce	25 mL
2 tbsp	lemon juice	25 mL
1 tbsp	lime juice	15 mL
1 tsp	packed brown sugar	5 mL
	Finely chopped cilantro (optional)	
	Hot white rice or noodles	

1. In a saucepan over medium heat, combine coconut milk and chili peppers. Bring to a simmer.

2. Add salmon and peas and cook, stirring, being careful not to let the mixture boil, about 3 minutes. Add fish sauce, lemon juice, lime juice and brown sugar and cook, stirring, for 1 minute. Taste for seasoning, adding more fish sauce, lemon or lime juice, or brown sugar, if desired.

3. Remove dried peppers, if using. Pour over rice or noodles. Garnish with cilantro, if using. Serve immediately.

> **MAXIMIZE CONVENIENCE**
> BY USING:
> ✦ Canned peas, drained, or frozen peas, cooked
> ✦ Bottled or frozen lemon juice
> ✦ Bottled lime juice
> ✦ Bottled preserved lemongrass

Parmesan-Crusted Snapper with Tomato Olive Sauce

Here's a quick and easy dish that takes advantage of the rich Mediterranean flavors of bottled antipasto sauce.

SERVES 4

Start to finish: 15 minutes

TIP: There are many kinds of antipasto sauce on the market. When making this recipe, check the label to ensure that it contains tomato and black olives.

EASY EXTRAS

✦ For a hint of spice, add a pinch of cayenne pepper to the bread crumb mixture.

✦ Stir 1 tbsp (15 mL) drained capers into antipasto sauce before serving.

1 cup	coarse dry bread crumbs, such as panko (see page 113)	250 mL
½ cup	grated Parmesan cheese	125 mL
½ tsp	salt	2 mL
	Freshly ground black pepper	
1 lb	snapper or other firm white fish fillets, patted dry, cut into 4 pieces	500 g
2 tbsp	mayonnaise	25 mL
1 tbsp	vegetable oil	15 mL
½ cup	bottled antipasto sauce (see Tip, left)	125 mL

1. In a bowl, combine bread crumbs, Parmesan, salt, and black pepper to taste. Spread mixture on a plate.

2. Brush fish evenly with mayonnaise, then dip in crumb mixture.

3. In a skillet, heat oil over medium heat. Add fish and cook, turning once, until it flakes easily when tested with a knife and outside is crisp and golden, about 3 minutes per side. Serve immediately topped with antipasto sauce.

Salmon Burgers

Nothing says lunch or a quick dinner better than a good burger. Here's a yummy fish-based version that can easily be varied with the addition of Easy Extras or by changing the toppings. To serve more, simply double or triple the recipe.

SERVES 2

Start to finish: 15 minutes

EASY EXTRAS

✦ Add ¼ cup (50 mL) finely chopped red or green onion to the salmon.

✦ Add 2 tbsp (25 mL) to ¼ cup (50 mL) finely chopped bell pepper or frozen mixed bell pepper strips, if desired, to the salmon in addition to or instead of the onion. If using frozen mixed pepper strips, remove them from the freezer before you start mixing.

✦ Garnish with a selection of lettuce, sliced tomato, sliced red onion and sliced red or yellow bell pepper.

1	can (7½ oz/213 g) salmon, drained	1
1	egg, beaten	1
½ cup	fine dry bread crumbs, divided	125 mL
1 tsp	dried Italian seasoning	5 mL
¼ tsp	salt	1 mL
	Freshly ground black pepper	
2 tbsp	vegetable oil	25 mL
2	onion or whole wheat buns, split and toasted	2
	Tartar sauce (see below)	

1. In a bowl, combine salmon, egg, ¼ cup (50 mL) of the bread crumbs, Italian seasoning, salt, and black pepper to taste. Mix well. Form mixture into 2 patties, about ½ inch (1 cm) thick. Spread remaining bread crumbs on a plate. Dip each patty into crumbs, covering both sides.

2. In a nonstick skillet, heat oil over medium heat. Add patties and cook, turning once, until hot and golden, about 3 minutes per side.

3. Serve on warm buns slathered with tartar sauce and add your favorite toppings.

TARTAR SAUCE

When I was growing up, tartar sauce, which usually contains capers and pickles as well as numerous seasonings, was the usual accompaniment for fish. I still like the combination and keep a jar in the fridge to embellish fish dishes. When I run out, I make this simplified version of the sauce.

Easy Tartar Sauce: In a bowl, combine ½ cup (125 mL) mayonnaise with 2 tbsp (25 mL) sweet green pickle relish. Stir to blend.

Potato Pancakes with Smoked Salmon

Potato pancakes, also known as latkes, are one of the world's great comfort foods. Topped with smoked salmon and a dollop of sour cream, they make an exquisite light meal.

SERVES 2

Start to finish: 25 minutes

TIPS: Give the batter a stir before cooking each batch.

If you prefer, use a food processor to mix the batter. Cut the potatoes into chunks and combine with the onion, egg, flour, salt and pepper. Add to food processor and pulse until combined. Don't overprocess or the mixture will be mush.

EASY EXTRAS

✦ Add ½ tsp (2 mL) paprika along with the flour.

✦ Garnish with finely chopped chives, dill, or green or red onion.

✦ PREHEAT OVEN TO 250°F (120°C)

1	can (19 oz/540 mL) whole white potatoes, drained, or 2 medium potatoes, cooked and peeled	1
½ cup	diced onion	125 mL
1	egg, beaten	1
1 tbsp	all-purpose flour	15 mL
½ tsp	salt	2 mL
	Freshly ground black pepper	
2 tbsp	vegetable oil (approx.)	25 mL
4	slices smoked salmon, thawed if frozen	4
	Sour cream	

1. Shred potatoes on coarse grater and finely chop any leftover bits.

2. In a bowl, combine potatoes, onion, egg, flour, salt, and black pepper to taste. Mix well. Shape into 4 small, thin pancakes.

3. In a nonstick skillet, heat oil over medium heat. Fry pancakes, in batches, turning once, until golden, about 3 minutes per side. Add more oil as required. Keep cooked pancakes warm in preheated oven.

4. To serve, place 2 pancakes on each plate. Top each with a piece of salmon and a dollop of sour cream.

Salmon Quiche

Here's a delightfully different weekday dinner or a great dish for a brunch or a buffet. Although it cooks for quite a while, it doesn't take long to prepare.

SERVES 4

Prep: 15 minutes
Baking: 40 to 45 minutes

TIPS: The quiche will bake more quickly if you are using a glass pie plate.

You can make this recipe using a blender instead of a food processor. To make the cracker crumbs, add the crackers to the blender in 2 or 3 batches and process. To make the batter, combine the cream cheese, eggs, milk and seasonings in the blender jug and process until integrated. (Stop the machine and scrape down the sides once or twice.) Gently stir the salmon, onion and roasted pepper into the mixture until combined. Proceed with Step 4.

EASY EXTRA

✦ Add ¼ cup (50 mL) finely chopped celery along with the salmon.

✦ PREHEAT OVEN TO 400°F (200°C)
✦ 9-INCH (23 CM) PIE PLATE

CRUST

30	cheese-flavored crackers, such as Ritz (about half an 8-oz/250 g box)	30
¼ cup	butter, melted	50 mL

FILLING

3 oz	cream cheese, cut into cubes and softened	90 g
3	eggs	3
1 cup	milk	250 mL
½ tsp	salt	2 mL
	Freshly ground black pepper	
1	can (7½ oz/213 g) salmon, including juice and bones, skin removed	1
¼ cup	chopped green onion, parsley or dill	50 mL
1	roasted red pepper, coarsely chopped	1

1. *Crust:* In a food processor or blender (see Tips, left), pulse crackers until they resemble coarse crumbs.

2. In a bowl, combine cracker crumbs and butter. Press into pie plate. Bake in preheated oven until golden, about 8 minutes. Reduce heat to 375°F (190°C).

3. *Filling:* In a food processor or blender, combine cream cheese and eggs. Process until smooth. Add milk, salt, and black pepper to taste and process until blended. Add salmon, green onion and roasted pepper and pulse two or three times until combined.

4. Pour salmon mixture into warm crust. Bake in preheated oven until filling is set, 40 to 45 minutes.

Pan-Fried Halibut in Spicy Lemon Sauce

I love the strong flavors in this bold sauce, which add zest and interest to a simple piece of fried fish. Serve with steamed broccoli and parsleyed potatoes for a traditional fish dinner with a difference.

SERVES 4

Start to finish: 15 minutes

TIP: If you are not using halibut in this recipe, be aware that other fish fillets are likely to be thinner. Cooking time will probably be closer to 3 minutes per side.

EASY EXTRA

✦ Stir in 1 tbsp (15 mL) drained capers along with the banana pepper.

✦ PREHEAT OVEN TO 250°F (120°C)

1 lb	halibut fillets or other firm white fish, such as snapper or sole, cut into 4 pieces (see Tip, left)	500 g
½ cup	all-purpose flour	125 mL
2 tbsp	vegetable oil	25 mL
1 tbsp	minced garlic	15 mL
1 cup	white wine	250 mL
½ cup	lemon juice	125 mL
1 tbsp	minced pickled banana pepper	15 mL
½ tsp	salt	2 mL
	Freshly ground black pepper	

1. Dip fish in flour to coat. Shake off and discard excess.

2. In a skillet, heat oil over medium heat. Add fish and cook, turning once, until cooked through and outside is crisp and golden, about 4 minutes per side, depending upon the thickness of the fish. Transfer to a warm platter and keep warm in preheated oven. Return pan to element.

3. Add garlic to pan and cook, stirring, for 1 minute. Add white wine and lemon juice and cook, stirring, until reduced by half, about 3 minutes. Stir in minced banana pepper, salt, and black pepper to taste. Pour over fish and serve.

Baked Fish with Tomatoes and Roasted Red Pepper

Nothing could be easier than this tasty bake, which is particularly delicious accompanied by fluffy mashed potatoes. Serve with a simple green salad for a complete meal.

SERVES 4

Start to finish: 25 minutes

TIP: If using frozen fish fillets in this recipe, thaw in the refrigerator during the day or in the microwave for about 6 minutes on Defrost power.

✦ PREHEAT OVEN TO 375°F (190°C)
✦ 6-CUP (1.5 L) SHALLOW BAKING DISH, LIGHTLY GREASED

1 lb	sole fillets or other firm white fish, such as snapper or halibut	500 g
20	cherry or grape tomatoes	20
½ cup	sliced roasted red pepper or 1 roasted red pepper, chopped	125 mL
⅓ cup	mayonnaise	75 mL
1 tbsp	Worcestershire sauce	15 mL
1 tbsp	Dijon mustard	15 mL
¼ tsp	salt	1 mL
	Freshly ground black pepper	
1 cup	dry bread crumbs	250 mL
2 tbsp	butter, melted	25 mL

1. In a microwave-safe dish, combine fish fillets with 2 tbsp (25 mL) water. Cover tightly with plastic wrap and microwave on High until fish flakes easily, about 3 minutes. (Or, in a skillet over medium heat, combine fish fillets with water to cover. Bring to a boil. Reduce heat to low and simmer until fish is just cooked through and flakes easily, about 5 minutes.) Using two forks, flake fish.

2. In prepared baking dish, combine fish, tomatoes and red pepper.

3. In a small bowl, whisk together mayonnaise, Dijon mustard, Worcestershire sauce, salt, and black pepper to taste. Spoon over fish mixture and stir to combine.

4. In a separate bowl, combine bread crumbs and butter. Sprinkle evenly over sauce. Bake in preheated oven until top is golden, about 15 minutes.

Paupiettes of Sole Florentine

Impress your guests with this elegant dish, which takes just minutes to make using bagged washed baby spinach and prepared Alfredo sauce. Serve with hot white rice and baby carrots for a great-tasting meal.

SERVES 4

Prep: 15 minutes
Baking: 15 minutes

TIP: If fillets are too wide to roll easily or to fit attractively on a plate, you will need to cut them in half lengthwise before proceeding with the recipe. Also, bear in mind that you will need 4 strips of sole to produce 4 roll-ups.

✦ PREHEAT OVEN TO 425°F (220°C)
✦ 6-CUP (1.5 L) SHALLOW BAKING DISH, LIGHTLY GREASED

1 lb	sole fillets, thawed if frozen and cut in half lengthwise, if necessary (see Tip, left)	500 g
2 tbsp	lemon juice	25 mL
1 tsp	paprika	5 mL
½ tsp	salt	2 mL
	Freshly ground black pepper	
1 cup	chopped baby spinach	250 mL
¼ cup	finely chopped green onion	50 mL
1 cup	prepared Alfredo sauce	250 mL

1. Sprinkle sole fillets evenly with lemon juice, paprika, salt, and black pepper to taste.

2. Sprinkle chopped baby spinach and green onion evenly over each fillet. Starting at narrow end, roll up, jelly roll style, and secure with a toothpick.

3. Place fish, seam side down, in prepared baking dish. Cover with Alfredo sauce. Bake in preheated oven until fish flakes easily with a fork, about 15 minutes. Remove toothpicks and serve immediately.

MAXIMIZE CONVENIENCE
BY USING:
✦ Bottled or frozen lemon juice
✦ Bagged washed baby spinach
✦ Prepared Alfredo sauce

Garlic Chili Shrimp

With a bag of shrimp in the freezer and two basic bottled Asian sauces, you can make this zesty Chinese-inspired dish at a moment's notice. I like to serve this on a small white oval platter to emphasize its simplicity. For a more colorful presentation, spread over a bed of lettuce leaves or sliced cucumber spiked with hot pepper flakes. Accompany with hot white rice.

SERVES 4

Start to finish: 10 minutes

EASY EXTRA

✦ Add 1 tsp (5 mL) cracked black peppercorns along with the garlic.

✦ SMALL PLATTER OR SERVING PLATE, LINED WITH LETTUCE LEAVES OR SLICED CUCUMBER (OPTIONAL)

1 tbsp	vegetable oil	15 mL
1 lb	peeled and deveined shrimp, thawed if frozen	500 g
1 tbsp	minced garlic	15 mL
2 tbsp	sweet sherry, sake or vodka	25 mL
2 tbsp	soy sauce	25 mL
1 to 2 tsp	Asian chili sauce (see page 142)	5 to 10 mL
2 tbsp	chopped green onion	25 mL

1. In a skillet, heat oil over medium-high heat. Add shrimp and cook, stirring, until they firm up and turn pink, 3 to 5 minutes. Using a slotted spoon, transfer to a platter or serving plate.

2. Add garlic to pan and cook, stirring, for 30 seconds. Add sherry, soy sauce and Asian chili sauce and stir until mixture boils, about 30 seconds. Pour over shrimp. Garnish with green onion and serve immediately.

SHRIMP

Virtually all shrimp sold today has been previously frozen, so there are few benefits to purchasing shrimp from a fish market. Bags of frozen shelled, cleaned shrimp, which can be kept in the freezer for as long as 2 months, are an indispensable convenience food. They should be thawed before cooking and not refrozen after thawing. Cook shrimp quickly over high heat for about 3 minutes. Cooking at too low a temperature produces a mushy texture, and overcooking makes them tough.

Shrimp in Tomato Sauce with Feta

I first had this dish many years ago when a friend served it at a dinner party. With its bold combination of flavors, this Greek specialty immediately catapulted to the top of my list of favorites. Since I love the taste of lemon, I prefer the addition of lemon zest. Serve over hot white rice.

SERVES 4

Start to finish: 15 minutes

EASY EXTRA

✦ Add 1 tsp (5 mL) grated lemon zest along with the lemon juice.

✦ PREHEAT BROILER
✦ 6-CUP (1.5 L) SHALLOW BAKING OR GRATIN DISH

2 tbsp	vegetable oil	25 mL
1 lb	peeled and deveined shrimp, thawed if frozen	500 g
2 tbsp	minced garlic	25 mL
	Freshly ground black pepper	
¼ cup	lemon juice	50 mL
1 cup	tomato sauce	250 mL
4 oz	crumbled feta cheese (about 1 cup/250 mL)	125 g

1. In a skillet, heat oil over medium-high heat. Add shrimp and cook, stirring, until they firm up and turn pink, 3 to 5 minutes. Using a slotted spoon, transfer to baking dish. Reduce heat to medium-low and return pan to element.

2. Add garlic, and black pepper to taste. Cook, stirring, for 1 minute. Add lemon juice and stir. Add tomato sauce and bring to a simmer.

3. Pour mixture over shrimp. Sprinkle with cheese. Place under preheated broiler until cheese begins to melt and turn brown, about 3 minutes.

MAXIMIZE CONVENIENCE
BY USING:
✦ Frozen peeled and deveined shrimp
✦ Bottled or frozen minced garlic
✦ Bottled or frozen lemon juice

Coconut Shrimp Curry

If you're lucky enough to have traveled to Thailand, you'll know that this is a version of the basic coconut milk curry that is served all over the country, but particularly in the south, where coconuts and shrimp are abundant. Many Thai cooks make their own curry paste, but bottled versions are now available in supermarkets with a well-stocked Asian foods section. This quick and easy recipe is delicious over hot white rice.

SERVES 4

Start to finish: 10 minutes

TIP: For a spicier version, increase the amount of curry paste. But be careful – a little goes a long way.

EASY EXTRAS

✦ Add 1 tsp (5 mL) grated lime zest along with the lime juice.

✦ Garnish with cilantro sprigs and/or red bell pepper strips.

1 tbsp	vegetable oil	15 mL
1 lb	peeled and deveined shrimp, thawed if frozen	500 g
	Freshly ground black pepper	
1 tbsp	red curry paste	15 mL
1 cup	coconut milk	250 mL
2 tbsp	fish sauce	25 mL
2 tbsp	lime juice	25 mL
1 tbsp	granulated sugar	15 mL
	Hot white rice	

1. In a skillet, heat oil over medium-high heat. Add shrimp and cook, stirring, until they firm up and turn pink, 3 to 5 minutes. Season with black pepper to taste. Using a slotted spoon, transfer to a deep platter and keep warm. Return pan to element.

2. Add red curry paste and cook, stirring, until it releases its aroma, 1 to 2 minutes. Stir in coconut milk, fish sauce, lime juice and sugar. Bring to a boil. Simmer for 1 to 2 minutes to combine flavors. Pour over shrimp.

3. Garnish with cilantro and red pepper strips, if desired (see Easy Extras). Serve immediately over hot white rice.

Creamy Corn and Shrimp

Quick, easy and delicious, this versatile casserole is great for dinner or as part of a buffet. Serve with fluffy white rice or pasta, accompanied by a simple green salad tossed in a vinaigrette dressing (see page 58).

SERVES 4

Start to finish: 20 minutes

EASY EXTRAS

✦ If you prefer a bit of spice, add a pinch of cayenne pepper to the shrimp, along with the paprika.

✦ Add ¼ cup (50 mL) finely chopped parsley to the corn mixture.

✦ PREHEAT OVEN TO 400°F (200°C)
✦ 6-CUP (1.5 L) BAKING DISH, GREASED

1 lb	cooked peeled shrimp, thawed if frozen, tails removed	500 g
2 tbsp	lemon juice	25 mL
1 tsp	paprika	5 mL
¼ tsp	freshly ground black pepper	1 mL
1	can (19 oz/540 mL) corn niblets, drained, or 2 cups (500 mL) cooked corn kernels	1
1 cup	prepared Alfredo sauce	250 mL
1	roasted red pepper, chopped	1
½ cup	finely chopped red or green onion	125 mL

1. In a bowl, combine shrimp, lemon juice, paprika and black pepper. Set aside.

2. In prepared baking dish, combine corn, Alfredo sauce, roasted red pepper and onion. Add shrimp and toss to combine.

3. Bake in preheated oven until hot and bubbling, about 15 minutes.

MAXIMIZE CONVENIENCE BY USING:

✦ Frozen cooked peeled shrimp
✦ Bottled or frozen lemon juice
✦ Bottled roasted red pepper
✦ Prepared Alfredo sauce

Poultry

It's not surprising that poultry is our favorite meat. Low in fat, high in protein and versatile, poultry combines well with many flavors and lends itself to many cooking techniques, from stir-fries to stews. Today, consumers can easily purchase a wide array of convenient poultry products, from fully cooked rotisserie chickens and sliced, cooked chicken breast to skinless, boneless parts (breasts, legs and thighs), quick-cooking cutlets and ground meat. There are many excellent brands of prepared chicken stock on the market, which add instant flavor to a variety of dishes.

When using cooked chicken in recipes, there are a number of options. Feel free to use cooked leftover chicken as well as precooked chicken from the supermarket or even cooked canned chicken, if you prefer. All work well in these recipes.

Chicken Provençal 108

Chicken Curry 109

Chinese Chicken. 110

Chicken and Artichoke Bake 112

Best-Ever Baked Chicken 113

Orange and Onion Chicken 114

Chicken and Black Bean Chili. 116

Spicy Peanut Chicken 117

Chicken Tacos 118

Italian-Style Chicken Cutlets 120

Turkey Sloppy Joes 121

Turkey Cutlets in Savory Cranberry Gravy 122

ON HAND

✓ Prepared chicken stock

✓ Frozen skinless boneless chicken parts (breast and/or thighs)

✓ Frozen ground chicken or turkey

✓ Frozen chicken or turkey cutlets

✓ Long-grain white rice

✓ Bottled tomato sauce

✓ Prepared bread crumbs

✓ A selection of frozen vegetables

✓ A selection of canned legumes

◄ Chicken Provençal

Chicken Provençal

Here's a quick version of an old classic. Instead of using bone-in chicken breasts, this recipe uses skinless boneless chicken breasts to speed up the cooking time. Serve with fluffy white rice and steamed broccoli.

SERVES 4

Start to finish: 25 minutes

TIPS: If using anchovy paste in this recipe, stir in after you have cooked the garlic.

For even greater convenience, use diced tomatoes, drained, in this recipe.

EASY EXTRAS

✦ Add ½ cup (125 mL) red or white wine to the pan after the garlic and Italian seasoning are cooked. Cook, stirring, until reduced by half about 3 minutes, then add the tomatoes.

✦ Add ½ cup (125 mL) sliced, pitted black olives after the sauce has thickened. Heat through before serving.

✦ Garnish with finely chopped parsley.

✦ PREHEAT OVEN TO 250°F (120°C)

1 lb	skinless boneless chicken breasts, sliced into ½-inch (1 cm) thick pieces, or 2 cooked small rotisserie chickens, quartered	500 g
2 tbsp	lemon juice	25 mL
½ cup	all-purpose flour	125 mL
2 tbsp	vegetable oil	25 mL
4	anchovies, chopped, or 4 tsp (20 mL) anchovy paste (see Tips, left)	4
1 tbsp	minced garlic	15 mL
1 tsp	dried Italian seasoning	5 mL
1	can (28 oz/796 mL) tomatoes, coarsely chopped, drained (see Tips, left)	1
	Salt and freshly ground black pepper	

1. If using skinless boneless chicken breasts, combine chicken pieces and lemon juice in a bowl. Stir to combine. Place flour in a resealable plastic bag. Add chicken mixture and toss until thoroughly and evenly coated with flour. In a skillet, heat oil over medium heat. Cook chicken, in batches, turning once, until golden outside and no longer pink inside, about 2 minutes per side. Transfer to heatproof dish and keep warm in preheated oven. (If using a cooked rotisserie chicken, reheat according to package instructions and keep warm in preheated oven. Heat 1 tbsp/15 mL oil over medium heat and proceed with Step 2.)

2. Add anchovies to skillet and cook, stirring, until dissolved. Add garlic and Italian seasoning and cook, stirring, for 1 minute. Add tomatoes and bring to boil. Reduce heat to low and simmer until sauce begins to thicken, about 5 minutes. Season with salt and black pepper to taste.

3. To serve, pour sauce into a deep platter or serving bowl. Lay chicken over top.

Chicken Curry

This delicious one-pan dinner is a great way to use up leftover chicken or to dress up a cooked rotisserie chicken.

SERVES 2

Start to finish: 15 minutes

TIP: To quickly cook the chicken for this recipe yourself, arrange 2 skinless boneless chicken breasts (thawed if frozen) in a single layer in a microwave-safe dish with 1/4 cup (50 mL) chicken stock or water. Cover tightly and microwave on High until the chicken is no longer pink inside, about 5 minutes. Let stand for at least 1 minute. (If covered with plastic wrap, puncture plastic with a sharp knife to let the steam escape.) Cut into 1-inch (2.5 cm) cubes and continue with recipe.

EASY EXTRAS

✦ Add 1/2 cup (125 mL) green peas and/or bell pepper strips along with the chicken.

✦ Stir in 1/4 cup (50 mL) whipping (35%) cream or 1/2 cup (125 mL) plain yogurt or 1/4 cup (50 mL) chutney just before serving.

1 tbsp	vegetable oil	15 mL
1/2 cup	diced onion	125 mL
1 tbsp	all-purpose flour	15 mL
2 tsp	curry powder	10 mL
1 cup	chicken stock	250 mL
2 cups	cubed (1 inch/2.5 cm) cooked chicken or 1 whole cooked chicken, cut into serving-size pieces, or 2 cans (each 10 oz/300 g) cut-up chicken	500 mL

Salt and freshly ground black pepper

Hot white rice or Indian bread

1. In a skillet, heat oil over medium heat. Add onion and cook, stirring, until softened, about 3 minutes.

2. Add flour and curry powder and cook, stirring, for 1 minute. Add stock and cook, stirring, until thickened, about 2 minutes.

3. Add chicken. Cover and simmer until chicken is heated through, about 5 minutes. (If you're using a cut-up rotisserie bone-in chicken, add 5 minutes to the heating time.) Season with salt and pepper to taste.

4. Serve over hot fluffy rice or with warm Indian bread such as naan or chapatti.

MAXIMIZE CONVENIENCE BY USING:

✦ Frozen diced onion

✦ Prepared chicken stock

✦ Canned or precooked chicken

Chinese Chicken

This tasty stir-fry takes advantage of quick-cooking skinless boneless chicken and frozen precut Chinese vegetables to minimize dinner preparation.

SERVES 4

Start to finish:
20 to 25 minutes

1 lb	skinless boneless chicken (breasts or thighs), cut into ½-inch (1 cm) slices	500 g
2 tbsp	soy sauce	25 mL
2 tbsp	sherry or white wine	25 mL
	Freshly ground black pepper	
2 tbsp	vegetable oil, divided	25 mL
1 tbsp	minced garlic	15 mL
1 lb	frozen precut vegetables for stir-fry	500 g
2 tbsp	hoisin sauce	25 mL
	Hot white rice	

1. In a bowl, combine chicken slices, soy sauce, sherry, and black pepper to taste. Set aside.

2. In a skillet, heat 1 tbsp (15 mL) of the oil over medium heat. Cook garlic and vegetables, stirring, until tender, about 6 minutes. Transfer to a bowl and keep warm.

3. Return skillet to medium heat and add remaining oil. Add reserved chicken mixture. Cook, stirring, until chicken is no longer pink inside, about 6 minutes. Add hoisin sauce and stir well to coat chicken. Add reserved vegetables and cook, stirring, until mixture is hot and steaming, about 2 minutes. Serve with hot white rice.

COOKING WHITE RICE

I learned to cook white rice from a Japanese friend many years ago, and her method is foolproof. All you need is a cast iron pot with a tight-fitting lid and an electric stove. In the pot, combine 1 cup (250 mL) white rice and 2 cups (500 mL) water. Bring to a boil over medium-high heat. Boil rapidly for 30 seconds. Cover tightly, turn off heat and let stand on warm element for 20 minutes.

Chicken and Artichoke Bake

This moist, tasty bake has a retro feel and a real hit of tomato flavor. It takes almost no time to prepare and is delicious over hot white rice.

SERVES 4

Start to finish: 30 minutes

TIP: If you don't have any green peas on hand, try substituting 1 cup (250 mL) black olives, drained, pitted and sliced, or 1 can (100 g/284 mL) sliced mushrooms, drained.

EASY EXTRA

✦ Add 2 tbsp (25 mL) finely chopped parsley to the bread crumb mixture in Step 2.

✦ PREHEAT OVEN TO 350°F (180°C)
✦ 6-CUP (1.5 L) BAKING DISH, GREASED

1	can (10 oz/284 mL) condensed cream of tomato soup, undiluted	1
½ cup	mayonnaise	125 mL
1 tbsp	lemon juice	15 mL
1 tbsp	Dijon mustard	15 mL
1 cup	dry bread crumbs	250 mL
2 tbsp	melted butter	25 mL
2 cups	cubed (½ inch/1 cm) or thinly sliced cooked chicken, or 2 cans (each 10 oz/300 g) cut-up chicken	500 mL
1	can (14 oz/398 mL) artichoke hearts, drained and quartered	1
1½ cups	green peas, thawed if frozen, or 1 can (14 oz/398 mL) green peas, drained (see Tip, left)	375 mL
2 tbsp	grated Parmesan cheese	25 mL

1. In a bowl, combine soup, mayonnaise, lemon juice and mustard. Set aside.

2. In a separate bowl, combine bread crumbs and butter.

3. In prepared baking dish, combine chicken, artichoke hearts, peas and reserved soup mixture. Mix to combine. Spread bread crumb mixture evenly over top. Sprinkle Parmesan cheese evenly over crumbs.

4. Bake in preheated oven until top is golden and mixture is bubbling, about 20 minutes.

MAXIMIZE CONVENIENCE
BY USING:
✦ Precooked chicken
✦ Prepared bread crumbs, such as panko
✦ Already grated Parmesan cheese

Best-Ever Baked Chicken

Requiring only about five minutes of preparation time, this crispy baked chicken is so easy and delicious that you'll never use a packaged mix again. In this recipe, I like to use panko, coarse packaged bread crumbs that create a particularly crunchy crust, but regular bread crumbs work well, too.

SERVES 4

Start to finish: 35 minutes

EASY EXTRA

✦ Add 2 tbsp (25 mL) finely chopped parsley to the bread crumb mixture in Step 2.

✦ PREHEAT OVEN TO 375°F (190°C)
✦ SHALLOW BAKING DISH

¼ cup	mayonnaise	50 mL
2 tbsp	prepared sun-dried tomato pesto	25 mL
4	skinless boneless chicken breasts (about 1 lb/500 g)	4
½ cup	bread or cracker crumbs	125 mL
¼ cup	grated Parmesan cheese	50 mL

1. In a small bowl, combine mayonnaise and pesto.

2. On a plate, combine bread crumbs and cheese. Brush chicken with mayonnaise mixture on all sides, then dip into crumbs to coat thoroughly.

3. Arrange chicken in a single layer in baking dish. Bake in preheated oven until no longer pink inside, about 30 minutes.

BREAD CRUMBS

It's easy to make bread crumbs in a food processor. Simply cut the bread into cubes and process until fine. To keep bread crumbs fresh, place them in a resealable bag, squeeze out all the air, seal and refrigerate or freeze. They will stay fresh for a week or so. If you need dry bread crumbs for a recipe, lightly toast the bread before processing. And, of course, you can always opt for convenience and purchase ready-made. The preferred bread crumbs are Japanese panko, which are quite coarse and produce a particularly crunchy crust. However, they can be a bit tricky to find as they are not always identified as such. They keep well; just store in a resealable bag after opening and use before the expiration date.

Orange and Onion Chicken

Use this recipe to dress up a rotisserie chicken or if you have leftover grilled or barbecued chicken. If you're cooking chicken, cook extra and refrigerate leftovers to make this tasty dish for dinner the following day. This is great with hot noodles or fluffy white rice.

SERVES 4

Start to finish: 20 minutes

TIP: Slicing the onion on the vertical produces nicely sized slices that look very attractive in this sauce. Peel the onion and slice it in half vertically. Lay the flat side down on a cutting board and cut thin crescent-shaped slices.

✦ PREHEAT OVEN TO 350°F (180°C)

2	small rotisserie chickens, quartered, or 1 lb (500 g) sliced cooked chicken breasts, or 4 grilled chicken breasts	2
1 tbsp	vegetable oil	15 mL
1	medium red onion, sliced on the vertical (see Tip, left)	1
1 cup	orange juice	250 mL
½ cup	orange marmalade	125 mL
1 tsp	soy sauce	5 mL
1 tbsp	cornstarch, dissolved in 2 tbsp (25 mL) water	15 mL

1. In a baking dish or microwave-safe dish, heat chicken until warm (see below if using rotisserie chicken).

2. In a skillet, heat oil over medium heat. Add onion and cook, stirring, until it begins to glaze, about 3 minutes. Add orange juice, orange marmalade and soy sauce. Cook, stirring, until marmalade dissolves and mixture reaches a simmer, about 3 minutes.

3. Add cornstarch mixture and stir just until it thickens (this will happen very quickly). Remove from heat, pour over warm chicken and serve immediately.

ROTISSERIE CHICKEN

Likely your supermarket has a rotisserie oven that cooks succulent chickens for you to take home. These tasty birds are a great convenience food, and you can increase their versatility by using them in some of these recipes. How you reheat a supermarket chicken is a matter of choice. You can place the chicken in an oven-to-table baking dish and warm in a preheated 350°F (180°C) oven for 15 minutes. Alternatively, microwave, covered, in a microwave-safe dish on High for about 5 minutes or until chicken is heated through.

Chicken and Black Bean Chili

Serve this tasty chili, which is lighter than one made with beef, with hot crusty bread and a steamed green vegetable.

SERVES 4

Start to finish: 20 minutes

1 tbsp	vegetable oil	15 mL
1 lb	skinless boneless chicken breasts, cut into 1/2-inch (1 cm) cubes	500 g
1 tbsp	minced garlic	15 mL
1 tbsp	chili powder	15 mL
1 tsp	cumin seeds, crushed	5 mL
1 1/2 cups	spicy tomato sauce, such as arrabbiata	375 mL
1	can (19 oz/540 mL) black beans, drained and rinsed	1
1 tbsp	lemon or lime juice	15 mL

1. In a skillet, heat oil over medium heat. Add chicken and cook, stirring, until it begins to brown and is no longer pink inside, about 3 minutes. Add garlic, chili powder and cumin seeds and cook, stirring, for 1 minute.

2. Add tomato sauce, beans and lemon juice. Stir to combine. Reduce heat to low and simmer for 10 minutes to allow flavors to combine.

VARIATION: Chicken, Sausage and Black Bean Chili: Stir in 4 oz (125 g) kielbasa, cut into 1/2-inch (1 cm) slices and quartered, along with the tomato sauce.

SKINLESS BONELESS CHICKEN

Skinless boneless chicken breasts and thighs and chicken (or turkey) cutlets are great time-savers, because they cook quickly, enabling you to enjoy the taste and versatility of freshly cooked chicken even on the busiest evenings. Buy them fresh and use before the expiration date or keep a supply in the freezer for maximum convenience. Thaw in the refrigerator overnight or in the microwave just before using.

Spicy Peanut Chicken

Surprise your family with this exotic stew, which is easily made with pantry ingredients. If you're a heat seeker, add the Asian chili sauce.

SERVES 4

Start to finish: 30 minutes

EASY EXTRA

✦ If you prefer a spicier result, add 1 tsp (5 mL) Asian chili sauce (see page 142) along with the peanut butter.

1 tbsp	vegetable oil	15 mL
1 lb	skinless boneless chicken, cut into 1-inch (2.5 cm) cubes	500 g
1 cup	diced onion	250 mL
1 tbsp	minced garlic	15 mL
2 tsp	curry powder	10 mL
1 tsp	salt	5 mL
	Freshly ground black pepper	
1 cup	chopped red or green bell pepper or 1½ cups (375 mL) frozen mixed bell pepper strips	250 mL
1 tbsp	all-purpose flour	15 mL
2 cups	tomato juice	500 mL
¼ cup	peanut butter	50 mL
	Hot white rice	

1. In a skillet, heat oil over medium heat. Add chicken and onion and cook, stirring, until onions are softened and chicken is no longer pink inside, about 8 minutes.

2. Add garlic, curry powder, salt, and black pepper to taste. Cook, stirring, for 1 minute. Add bell pepper and cook, stirring, for 1 minute. Add flour and cook, stirring, for 1 minute.

3. Add tomato juice. Bring to a boil. Cook, stirring, until thickened, about 5 minutes. Add peanut butter and stir until blended. Serve over hot white rice.

MAXIMIZE CONVENIENCE
BY USING:
✦ Frozen diced onion
✦ Bottled or frozen minced garlic
✦ Frozen mixed bell pepper strips

Chicken Tacos

Kids love this tactile dish, and adults enjoy its Tex-Mex flavors and ease of preparation. I've kept the spicing mild to appeal to young palates, but the heat is easily bumped up with the addition of a jalapeño or chipotle pepper, or spicy salsa as a garnish.

SERVES 4

Start to finish: 20 minutes

TIPS: If desired, use 8 oz (250 g) precooked sliced chicken breast or 1 can (10 oz/300 g) cut-up chicken in this recipe. Chop and add to the pan along with the beans.

The consistency of refried beans varies among brands. If yours are almost solid when removed from the can, you may need to add as much as 1/4 cup (50 mL) water along with the beans to facilitate integration of the ingredients.

EASY EXTRA

✦ For a spicier result, add 1 finely chopped jalapeño pepper or chipotle pepper in adobo sauce along with the chili powder.

1 tbsp	vegetable oil	15 mL
8 oz	skinless boneless chicken breasts, cut into 1/2-inch (1 cm) cubes (see Tips, left)	250 g
1/2 tsp	chili powder	2 mL
	Freshly ground black pepper	
1 cup	drained canned corn kernels or thawed corn kernels	250 mL
1	roasted red pepper, finely chopped	1
1	can (14 oz/398 mL) refried beans (see Tips, left)	1
1 cup	shredded Tex-Mex cheese mix or Monterey Jack cheese	250 mL
12	taco shells	12
	Salsa	
	Shredded lettuce	
	Chopped tomato	
	Finely chopped red or green onion	
	Cubed avocado	
	Sour cream	

1. In a skillet, heat oil over medium heat. Add chicken and cook, stirring, until lightly browned and no longer pink inside, about 5 minutes. Sprinkle with chili powder, and black pepper to taste. Cook, stirring, for 1 minute. Add corn, red pepper and beans and bring to a boil.

2. Reduce heat to low and simmer for 2 to 3 minutes. Add cheese and stir until melted.

3. Warm taco shells according to package directions. Fill with bean mixture and garnish with any combination of salsa, lettuce, tomato, onion, avocado and/or sour cream.

Italian-Style Chicken Cutlets

Chicken and turkey cutlets are a great mealtime solution as they cook very quickly. Here's a fresh-tasting dish that takes no time to prepare. Serve with fluffy white rice or crisp hash brown potatoes.

SERVES 4

Start to finish: 20 minutes

TIP: Substitute turkey cutlets for the chicken, if desired.

EASY EXTRA

✦ Add 4 slices prosciutto, chopped, along with the tomato sauce.

✦ PREHEAT OVEN TO 250°F (120°C)

1 lb	chicken breast cutlets	500 g
¼ cup	lemon juice	50 mL
¼ cup	all-purpose flour	50 mL
1 tsp	dried Italian seasoning	5 mL
½ tsp	freshly ground black pepper	2 mL
2 tbsp	vegetable oil, divided	25 mL
2 cups	washed baby spinach	500 mL
1 cup	tomato sauce	250 mL
2 tbsp	grated Parmesan cheese	25 mL

1. Dip each cutlet in lemon juice until coated. On a plate, combine flour, Italian seasoning, and black pepper to taste. Dip chicken into flour mixture to coat evenly on both sides, shaking off and discarding excess.

2. In a skillet, heat 1 tbsp (15 mL) of the oil over medium-high heat. Sauté chicken, in batches if necessary, until browned outside and no longer pink inside, 2 to 3 minutes per side. Transfer to a platter and keep warm in preheated oven while making the sauce.

3. Reduce heat to medium-low and add remaining oil to pan, if necessary. Add spinach and cook, stirring, until wilted. Add tomato sauce. Bring to a boil and cook, stirring, for 1 minute. Add Parmesan and stir until cheese melts. Pour sauce over chicken and serve immediately.

> **MAXIMIZE CONVENIENCE**
> BY USING:
> ✦ Bottled or frozen lemon juice
> ✦ Bagged washed baby spinach
> ✦ Prepared tomato sauce
> ✦ Already grated Parmesan cheese

Turkey Sloppy Joes

Here's a kid-friendly meal that is ideal for busy evenings. Add the cream cheese if you prefer a more mellow mixture or if you need to stretch the recipe to feed an extra person. Open a bag of mixed salad greens, add some chopped green onion and toss with a simple dressing for a nutritious and satisfying meal.

SERVES 4

Start to finish: 20 minutes

EASY EXTRAS

✦ Add ½ cup (125 mL) diced celery along with the turkey.

✦ Add 1 cup (250 mL) chopped bell pepper or 1½ cups (375 mL) frozen mixed bell pepper strips along with the garlic.

1 cup	tomato-based chili sauce	250 mL
1 tbsp	Dijon mustard	15 mL
1 tbsp	Worcestershire sauce	15 mL
1 tbsp	vegetable oil	15 mL
1 lb	lean ground turkey or chicken	500 g
1 cup	diced onion	250 mL
1 tbsp	minced garlic	15 mL
½ tsp	salt	2 mL
	Freshly ground black pepper	
4 oz	cream cheese (optional)	125 g
	Toasted onion or hamburger buns	

1. In a bowl, combine chili sauce, mustard and Worcestershire sauce. Set aside.

2. In a skillet, heat oil over medium heat. Add turkey and onion and cook, stirring and breaking up turkey until no longer pink inside and onion is softened, about 5 minutes. Add garlic, salt, and black pepper to taste. Cook, stirring, for 1 minute. Stir in reserved sauce and bring to boil.

3. Reduce heat to low. Add cream cheese, if using. Simmer for 10 minutes or until cheese is melted and flavors are combined. Spoon over toasted buns.

MAXIMIZE CONVENIENCE
BY USING:

✦ Frozen diced onion
✦ Bottled or frozen minced garlic

Turkey Cutlets in Savory Cranberry Gravy

Here's a great recipe for a holiday dinner if you don't feel like cooking an entire bird. It's absolutely delicious, attractive and will elicit compliments from the first bite. That said, it is also speedy enough for a quick weeknight meal served over fluffy white rice.

SERVES 4

Start to finish: 20 minutes

TIPS: If you prefer a sauce with a bit more tartness, increase cider vinegar to 2 tbsp (25 mL).

Substitute chicken cutlets for the turkey if you prefer.

EASY EXTRA

✦ If you prefer a bit of spice, add as much as ¼ tsp (1 mL) cayenne pepper to the flour mixture.

✦ PREHEAT OVEN TO 250°F (120°C)

¼ cup	all-purpose flour	50 mL
½ tsp	salt	2 mL
Pinch	freshly ground black pepper	Pinch
1 lb	turkey breast cutlets	500 g
2 tbsp	vegetable oil, divided	25 mL
½ cup	chicken stock or water	125 mL
1 tbsp	cider vinegar	15 mL
2 tbsp	packed brown sugar	25 mL
1 tbsp	Dijon mustard	15 mL
1	can (14 oz/398 mL) cranberry sauce, preferably whole berry	1

1. On a plate, combine flour, salt and black pepper. Dip turkey into flour mixture to coat evenly on both sides, shaking off excess.

2. In a skillet, heat 1 tbsp (15 mL) of the oil over medium-high heat. Sauté turkey, in batches, adding more oil as necessary, until golden outside and no longer pink inside, 2 to 3 minutes per side. Transfer to a deep platter and keep warm in preheated oven while making the sauce.

3. Add chicken stock and cider vinegar to pan. Cook, stirring and scraping pan to loosen any brown bits, until mixture is reduced by half, about 2 minutes. Add brown sugar and mustard and stir until blended. Stir in cranberry sauce and bring to a boil. Pour over cutlets and serve immediately.

Beef, Pork and Lamb

Along with poultry, beef, pork and lamb are our main sources of high-quality protein and iron. Not only are these meats versatile — suitable for both casual weekday meals and elegant dinners — they can be cooked with an almost unlimited combination of vegetables, herbs and even fruit. The easy-to-prepare dishes in this chapter take advantage of ground meats and the more tender cuts, which cook quickly. The use of prepared soups and sauces and other convenience foods helps to create hearty and delicious dinners in a flash.

Crispy Shepherd's Pie.......................... 126

Salisbury Steak with Mushroom Gravy........... 127

Chinese Pepper Steak 128

Chili con Carne Pronto 130

Beef and Broccoli with Rice Stick Noodles....... 131

Steak Creole 132

Beef Stroganoff............................... 134

Red Flannel Hash 135

Beans, Beef and Biscuits....................... 136

Sausage and Black Bean Chili 138

Sausage Polenta Lasagna 139

Sausage and Red Pepper Risotto 140

East-West Chili Pork 142

Savory Lamb Chops........................... 143

Just Peachy Pork 144

ON HAND

- ✓ Frozen beef for stir-fry
- ✓ Frozen ground beef
- ✓ Frozen pork tenderloin
- ✓ Frozen Italian sausage
- ✓ Frozen lamb chops
- ✓ Prepared beef stock
- ✓ Dijon mustard
- ✓ Worcestershire sauce
- ✓ Tomato ketchup
- ✓ Tomato-based chili sauce

Crispy Shepherd's Pie

Shepherd's pie has a long and noble history, dating back to the 18th century, when it was simple fare served to shepherds. It is traditionally made with a mashed potato crust, but this version takes advantage of frozen hash brown potatoes to produce a crispy and more convenient topping.

SERVES 4

Start to finish: 30 minutes

EASY EXTRA

✦ Add 1 1/2 cups (375 mL) canned corn kernels, drained, frozen corn kernels, thawed, or cooked corn kernels along with the ketchup.

✦ PREHEAT OVEN TO 375°F (190°C)
✦ 9-INCH (23 CM) PIE PLATE

2 tbsp	vegetable oil, divided	25 mL
2 cups	frozen hash brown potatoes	500 mL
1 lb	lean ground beef, thawed if frozen	500 g
1 cup	diced onion	250 mL
1 tbsp	minced garlic	15 mL
1/4 tsp	salt	1 mL
	Freshly ground black pepper	
2 tbsp	all-purpose flour	25 mL
1 cup	beef stock	250 mL
1/2 cup	ketchup	125 mL
1 tbsp	Worcestershire sauce	15 mL

1. In a skillet, heat 1 tbsp (15 mL) of the oil over medium-high heat. Add potatoes and cook, stirring, until crisp, about 7 minutes. Using a slotted spoon, transfer to a paper towel-lined plate to drain.

2. Add remaining oil to pan. Add beef and onion and cook, breaking up meat, until beef is no longer pink inside, about 5 minutes. Drain off fat.

3. Return pan to element. Add garlic, salt, and black pepper to taste. Cook, stirring, for 1 minute. Add flour and cook, stirring, for 1 minute. Add beef stock and bring to a boil. Cook, stirring, until mixture thickens, 3 minutes. Stir in ketchup and Worcestershire sauce and return to a boil.

4. Pour mixture into pie plate. Sprinkle potatoes over top. Bake in preheated oven until mixture is hot and bubbling, about 10 minutes.

MAXIMIZE CONVENIENCE
BY USING:
✦ Frozen ground beef, thawed
✦ Frozen diced onion
✦ Bottled or frozen minced garlic
✦ Prepared beef stock

Salisbury Steak with Mushroom Gravy

Salisbury steak is a flavored meat patty that is smothered in pan gravy. I like to serve this with mounds of fluffy mashed potatoes to soak up the flavorful sauce.

SERVES 4

Start to finish: 25 minutes

TIPS: *To make your own beef patties:* In a bowl, combine 1 lb (500 g) lean ground beef, 1 cup (250 mL) diced onion, ½ cup (125 mL) dry bread crumbs, 2 tsp (10 mL) dried Italian seasoning, ½ tsp (2 mL) salt and ¼ tsp (1 mL) freshly ground black pepper. Mix well and form into 4 patties of uniform size, about ½ inch (1 cm) thick. Place ½ cup (125 mL) bread crumbs on a plate. Dip patties in crumbs to coat evenly and proceed with Step 2.

If you are using frozen beef patties in this recipe and have difficulty getting the crumb mixture to adhere to the meat, dip the patties in beaten egg before coating with crumbs.

½ cup	dry bread crumbs	125 mL
2 tsp	dried Italian seasoning	10 mL
	Freshly ground black pepper	
4	frozen beef patties (each 4 oz/125 g) or 1 lb (500 g) lean ground beef, thawed if frozen (see Tips, left)	4
1 tbsp	vegetable oil	15 mL
8 oz	sliced mushrooms	250 g
½ cup	sherry, white wine or water	125 mL
½ cup	water	125 mL
1	can (10 oz/284 mL) condensed cream of mushroom soup	1
1 tbsp	Worcestershire sauce	15 mL

1. On a plate, mix together bread crumbs, Italian seasoning, and black pepper to taste. Dip each patty into crumb mixture, coating evenly on both sides (see Tips, left).

2. In a skillet, heat oil over medium-high heat. Add patties and cook until no longer pink inside, 4 to 7 minutes per side depending upon thickness. Transfer to a deep platter and keep warm while making the gravy. Drain off all but 1 tbsp (15 mL) fat from pan.

3. Add mushrooms and cook, stirring, until they begin to brown and lose their liquid, about 7 minutes. Add sherry and water and cook, stirring, for 1 minute, scraping up any brown bits from bottom of pan. Add mushroom soup and stir well to remove lumps. Bring to a boil. Reduce heat to low and simmer for 2 minutes. Stir in Worcestershire sauce. Taste and adjust seasoning. Pour over cooked patties and serve.

Chinese Pepper Steak

This recipe takes advantage of bottled Asian sauces to create a great-tasting dinner that is appetizing enough to share with guests. Add the Asian chili sauce (see Easy Extras, below) if you like a bit of heat. Serve over hot noodles or fluffy white rice.

SERVES 4

Start to finish: 15 minutes

EASY EXTRAS

✦ Add 2 tbsp (25 mL) vodka along with the bell pepper.

✦ If you like a bit of heat, stir in 1 tsp (5 mL) or to taste, Asian chili sauce (see page 142) after the sauce has thickened.

1 tbsp	vegetable oil	15 mL
1 lb	thinly sliced beef sirloin or stir-fry strips	500 g
1 tbsp	minced garlic	15 mL
1 tbsp	minced gingerroot	15 mL
1/2 tsp	cracked black peppercorns	2 mL
1 cup	diced red or green bell pepper or 1 1/2 cups (375 mL) frozen mixed bell pepper strips	250 mL
1/2 cup	beef stock	125 mL
2 tbsp	soy sauce	25 mL
1 tbsp	hoisin sauce	15 mL
1 tbsp	cornstarch, dissolved in 2 tbsp (25 mL) water	15 mL
2 tbsp	finely chopped green onion	25 mL

1. In a skillet, heat oil over medium-high heat. Add steak and cook, stirring, until it begins to brown and there is no hint of red, 2 to 3 minutes. Transfer to a warm platter and keep warm.

2. Reduce heat to medium. Add garlic, ginger and peppercorns and cook, stirring, for 1 minute. Add bell pepper and cook, stirring, for 1 minute. Add beef stock, soy sauce and hoisin sauce. Bring to a boil.

3. Add cornstarch mixture and cook, stirring, until thickened, about 2 minutes. Pour over beef. Garnish with green onion and serve immediately.

> **MAXIMIZE CONVENIENCE**
> BY USING:
> ✦ Presliced beef for stir-fry
> ✦ Bottled or frozen minced garlic
> ✦ Bottled minced gingerroot
> ✦ Prepared beef stock

Chili con Carne Pronto

Here's a tasty old-fashioned chili that is quick and easy to make. Serve with hot buttered toast. If you prefer a spicier version, add a jalapeño or chipotle pepper (see Easy Extras, below).

SERVES 4

Start to finish: 20 minutes

TIP: If you have celery in your crisper, substitute 2 stalks, peeled and diced, for the celery seed. Cook with the onion and beef, until the celery is softened, about 6 minutes.

EASY EXTRAS

✦ Add ½ cup (125 mL) diced bell pepper along with the garlic.

✦ For a spicier version, add 1 finely chopped jalapeño pepper or, if you prefer a bit of smoke, 1 finely chopped chipotle pepper in adobo sauce along with the garlic.

1 tbsp	vegetable oil	15 mL
1 lb	lean ground beef, thawed if frozen	500 g
1 cup	diced onion	250 mL
1 tbsp	minced garlic	15 mL
1 tbsp	chili powder	15 mL
½ tsp	celery seed (see Tip, left)	2 mL
2 cups	spicy tomato sauce, such as arrabbiata	500 mL
1	can (19 oz/540 mL) kidney beans, drained and rinsed	1

1. In a skillet, heat oil over medium-high heat. Add beef and onion and cook, breaking up meat with a spoon, until beef is no longer pink inside, about 5 minutes. Add garlic, chili powder and celery seed and cook, stirring, for 1 minute. Add tomato sauce and beans. Bring to a boil.

2. Reduce heat to low and simmer until beans are heated through and flavors are combined, about 10 minutes.

CELERY SEED

Because it is an easy way to impart a celery flavor to soups and stews, I like to keep dried celery seed in my pantry. However, it has a very strong taste, which some people don't like. It should be used cautiously as it can easily overpower a dish, leaving an unpleasant bitterness. It is not to be confused with celery salt, which is usually a blend of ground celery seed, salt and other herbs.

Beef and Broccoli with Rice Stick Noodles

Here's a tasty stir-fry that uses dried rice noodles, which don't need to be cooked. Just cover with boiling water until they soften to the desired consistency. Dried rice noodles are widely available in Asian grocery stores and supermarkets, but pasta, such as spaghetti, fettuccine and egg noodles, cooked according to package instructions also works well in this recipe.

SERVES 4

Start to finish: 20 minutes

TIP: Sliced beef for stir-fries is widely available in supermarkets. It can be purchased fresh or frozen. If frozen, thaw before using in this recipe.

EASY EXTRAS

✦ Add 2 tbsp (25 mL) chopped, drained water chestnuts along with the broccoli.

✦ Garnish with 1 tbsp (15 mL) toasted sesame seeds or 1 fresh red chili pepper, thinly sliced.

✦ Add a garnish of finely chopped green onion.

✦ WOK OR NONSTICK SKILLET

8 oz	thick rice noodles	250 g
2 tbsp	vegetable oil, divided	25 mL
3 cups	broccoli florets	750 mL
6 tbsp	soy sauce	90 mL
2 tbsp	vodka, beef stock or water	25 mL
1 tbsp	minced garlic	15 mL
1 tbsp	minced gingerroot	15 mL
1 tbsp	cornstarch, dissolved in 2 tbsp (25 mL) water	15 mL
1 tsp	granulated sugar	5 mL
	Freshly ground black pepper	
12 oz	thinly sliced sirloin steak or stir-fry strips (see Tip, left)	375 g
1 tsp	sesame oil	5 mL

1. Soak rice noodles in a bowl of boiling water for 10 minutes. Drain and toss with 1 tbsp (15 mL) of the oil. Set aside.

2. In a pot of boiling salted water, cook broccoli florets for 3 minutes. Drain and set aside.

3. Meanwhile, in a bowl, combine soy sauce, vodka, garlic, ginger, cornstarch mixture, sugar, and black pepper to taste. Set aside.

4. In a wok or nonstick skillet, heat remaining oil over medium heat. Add beef and cook, stirring, until cooked through, about 4 minutes. Add reserved soy sauce mixture and cook, stirring, until beef is well coated and mixture thickens, about 2 minutes. Add broccoli and cook, stirring, for 1 minute. Stir in reserved noodles and cook until heated through and well coated with sauce, about 2 minutes. Sprinkle with sesame oil and serve immediately.

Steak Creole

What could make a better Sunday dinner or weekend supper in the country than steak bathed in an abundance of rich, flavorful gravy? Serve this with mounds of fluffy mashed potatoes to soak up the sauce.

SERVES 6

Start to finish: 30 minutes

TIP: If you don't have celery in the refrigerator, use ¼ tsp (1 mL) celery seed instead; add along with the garlic.

✦ PREHEAT OVEN TO 250°F (120°C)

2 lbs	sirloin steak (about 1 inch/2.5 cm thick)	1 kg
1 tbsp	Cajun seasoning or paprika	15 mL
1 tbsp	vegetable oil	15 mL
1 cup	diced onion	250 mL
½ cup	diced celery (see Tip, left)	125 mL
1 cup	diced green bell pepper or 1½ cups (375 mL) frozen mixed bell pepper strips	250 mL
1 tbsp	minced garlic	15 mL
1 tbsp	all-purpose flour	15 mL
¾ cup	ketchup	175 mL
¾ cup	beef stock or water	175 mL
1 tbsp	Worcestershire sauce	15 mL
1 tbsp	grainy mustard	15 mL
	Salt and freshly ground black pepper	

1. Pat steak dry with paper towel and rub both sides with Cajun seasoning.

2. In a skillet, heat oil over medium-high heat. Add steak and cook until desired doneness, about 6 minutes per side for medium. Transfer to a deep platter and keep warm in preheated oven.

3. Reduce heat to medium. Add onion and celery to pan and cook, stirring, until celery is softened, about 6 minutes. Add green pepper and garlic and cook, stirring, for 1 minute. Add flour and cook, stirring, for 1 minute. Add ketchup, beef stock and Worcestershire sauce and cook, stirring, until mixture thickens, about 5 minutes. Stir in mustard. Season with salt and black pepper to taste. Pour over warm steaks and serve immediately. Slice steak at table.

Beef Stroganoff

Here's a dish that is quick to make yet elegant enough for special occasions. The sauce is delicious over hot buttered egg noodles. Just add a bottle of robust red wine and a crisp green salad.

SERVES 4

Start to finish: 30 minutes

EASY EXTRAS

✦ Add ¼ cup (50 mL) vodka to pan before adding the flour and cook, stirring, for 1 minute.

✦ Add 1 tsp (5 mL) paprika along with the flour.

✦ Garnish with finely chopped dill or dill sprigs.

✦ PREHEAT OVEN TO 250°F (120°C)

1 tbsp	vegetable oil	15 mL
2 tbsp	butter, divided	25 mL
8 oz	sliced mushrooms	250 g
1 lb	sirloin steak, cut into ½-inch (1 cm) slices	500 g
¼ tsp	salt	1 mL
	Freshly ground black pepper	
2 tbsp	minced shallots or finely chopped green onion (white part only)	25 mL
1 tbsp	all-purpose flour	15 mL
1 cup	beef stock	250 mL
1 tbsp	Dijon mustard	15 mL
½ cup	sour cream	125 mL
1	dill pickle, finely chopped	1
	Hot buttered egg noodles	

1. In a skillet, heat oil and 1 tbsp (15 mL) of the butter over medium-high heat. Add mushrooms and cook, stirring, until they begin to lose their liquid, about 7 minutes. Using a slotted spoon, transfer to a plate and keep warm in preheated oven.

2. Add remaining butter to pan. Add steak slices and sauté until desired degree of doneness, about 1½ minutes per side for medium. Season with salt, and black pepper to taste. Transfer to a warm platter and keep warm in oven.

3. Reduce heat to medium. Add shallots to pan and cook, stirring, for 1 minute. Add flour and cook, stirring, for 1 minute. Add stock. Bring to a boil. Cook, stirring, until thickened, about 3 minutes. Stir in mustard.

4. Return mushrooms to pan. Add sour cream and chopped dill pickle and cook, stirring, just until cream is heated through, about 1 minute. (Do not let mixture boil or it will curdle.) Pour over steak and serve with hot noodles.

Red Flannel Hash

Traditionally a way of using up the leftovers from a boiled dinner containing corned beef and beets, over the years this dish has acquired a life of its own. I like to serve this topped with a poached egg (see page 72) and accompanied by a simple green salad.

SERVES 4 TO 6

Start to finish: 30 minutes

TIPS: For added convenience, use a food processor to chop the ingredients for this recipe. Add in batches and pulse until desired consistency is reached.

◆ PREHEAT BROILER
◆ OVENPROOF SKILLET WITH HEATPROOF HANDLE (SEE TIP, PAGE 71)

10 oz	chopped corned beef	300 g
1	can (19 oz/540 mL) potatoes, drained and diced, or 2 cups (500 mL) cooked potatoes, diced	1
1	can (14 oz/398 mL) sliced beets, drained and diced, or 2 cups (500 mL) diced cooked beets	1
¼ cup	dry bread crumbs	50 mL
¼ cup	cream or milk	50 mL
2 tbsp	butter	25 mL
1 cup	chopped onion	250 mL
1 tsp	dried oregano leaves	5 mL
	Freshly ground black pepper	
	Poached eggs (optional)	
	Onion relish, tomato chutney or tomato-based chili sauce	

1. In a bowl, combine chopped corned beef, potatoes, beets, bread crumbs and cream. Mix well.

2. In an ovenproof skillet, heat butter over medium-low heat. Add onion and cook, stirring, until softened, about 4 minutes. Add oregano, and black pepper to taste. Cook, stirring, for 1 minute. Stir in corned beef mixture.

3. Using a spatula, push mixture down into pan, flattening and smoothing top. Cook, without stirring, until it forms a crust on the bottom, about 8 minutes. Place under broiler until the top is crispy, about 8 minutes.

4. To serve, cut into wedges and top with a poached egg, if desired. Accompany with onion relish, chutney or chili sauce.

Beans, Beef and Biscuits

Topped with hot biscuits, this hearty mix looks as good as it tastes. Serve with a tossed green salad for a great family meal.

SERVES 6

Start to finish: 30 minutes

TIPS: Placing the biscuits on a hot filling prevents them from becoming mushy on the bottom during baking.

Arrabbiata is my favorite spicy tomato sauce.

✦ PREHEAT OVEN TO 375°F (190°C)
✦ 8-CUP (2 L) BAKING DISH, LIGHTLY GREASED

1 tbsp	vegetable oil	15 mL
1 lb	lean ground beef, thawed if frozen	500 g
1 cup	diced onion	250 mL
½ cup	finely chopped celery	125 mL
2 cups	spicy tomato sauce	500 mL
2	cans (each 14 oz/398 mL) baked beans in tomato sauce	2
1 tbsp	Worcestershire sauce	15 mL
1	can (8 oz/250 g) country-style biscuit dough	1

1. In a skillet, heat oil over medium heat. Add beef, onion and celery and cook, breaking up meat with a spoon, until beef is no longer pink and vegetables are softened, about 7 minutes. Add tomato sauce, baked beans and Worcestershire sauce and bring to a boil. Reduce heat to low and simmer for 2 minutes. Pour into prepared dish.

2. Separate dough into individual biscuits. Arrange evenly over top of bean mixture (there will be spaces in between). Bake in preheated oven until biscuits are puffed and brown, 10 to 12 minutes. Serve immediately.

CELERY

Celery is one of nature's convenience foods. Available year-round, it is very versatile and if stored in a vented plastic bag will keep for about a week in the crisper. Its slightly salty flavor complements a wide variety of foods and makes celery a useful crudité. It adds crunch to salads and flavor to soups and stews. If you run out of parsley, use celery leaves as a garnish instead. When purchasing celery, choose heads that are firm and tight, with ribs that snap easily, and avoid any that seem woody. When it begins to pass its peak, break off the ribs and refresh in a bowl of ice water for 30 minutes.

Sausage and Black Bean Chili

This nutritious family dinner is packed with flavor and ready in no time. It's delicious over hot white rice or with crusty rolls, accompanied by a crisp green salad.

SERVES 4

Start to finish: 25 minutes

TIPS: If you prefer a less spicy version of this dish, substitute 1 green bell pepper, thinly sliced, or 1 cup (250 mL) frozen mixed bell pepper strips for the jalapeño.

Use hot or sweet Italian sausage, depending upon your preference.

EASY EXTRA

✦ Add 1 green bell pepper, thinly sliced, or 1 cup (250 mL) frozen mixed bell pepper strips along with the jalapeño.

1 lb	Italian sausage, removed from casings	500 g
1 cup	diced onion	250 mL
1 to 2	jalapeño peppers, finely chopped (see Tips, left)	1 to 2
½ tsp	salt	2 mL
	Freshly ground black pepper	
¾ cup	tomato-based chili sauce	175 mL
2 tbsp	Dijon mustard	25 mL
1 tbsp	Worcestershire sauce	15 mL
1	can (19 oz/540 mL) black beans, drained and rinsed	1

1. In a skillet over medium heat, cook sausage, breaking up with a spoon, until lightly browned and no longer pink inside, about 5 minutes. Drain off all but 1 tbsp (15 mL) fat.

2. Add onion to pan and cook, stirring, until softened, about 3 minutes. Add jalapeño pepper, salt, and black pepper to taste. Cook, stirring, for 1 minute. Add chili sauce, Dijon mustard and Worcestershire sauce. Bring to a boil. Stir in beans.

3. Reduce heat to low and simmer until mixture is bubbling and flavors are combined, about 10 minutes. Taste and adjust seasoning.

SAUSAGES

Sausages, which are usually made from a seasoned ground meat mixture stuffed into casings, are a quick way of adding interesting flavors to many dishes. They can speed up food preparation because the chopping, seasoning and sometimes even cooking have already been completed. Uncooked or cured, they are widely available in many different forms. Uncooked sausage cooks quickly and blends well with a wide variety of foods. Fresh uncooked sausage will keep for 3 days in the refrigerator and can be frozen for as long as 2 months.

Sausage Polenta Lasagna

Here's a version of lasagna that uses prepared tomato sauce, Italian sausage and ready-made polenta to take the work out of this normally labor-intensive dish. Use hot or mild Italian sausage, depending upon your preference. This is very rich and filling, so all you need to add is a simple salad.

SERVES 4

Start to finish: 30 minutes

TIP: I use a small oval baking dish when making this recipe; it accommodates the polenta in two layers. If a square dish is used, the assembly may vary, possibly requiring additional layers.

✦ PREHEAT OVEN TO 350°F (180°C)
✦ 6-CUP (1.5 L) BAKING DISH, LIGHTLY GREASED

1 tbsp	vegetable oil	15 mL
1 lb	Italian sausage, removed from casings	500 g
2 cups	tomato sauce	500 mL
1	polenta roll (1 lb/500 g), cut into ½-inch (1 cm) thick slices	1
1 cup	shredded mozzarella cheese	250 mL
2 tbsp	grated Parmesan cheese	25 mL

1. In a skillet, heat oil over medium heat. Add sausage and cook, breaking up with a spoon, until lightly browned and no longer pink, about 5 minutes. Drain off fat. Add tomato sauce. Reduce heat to low and simmer for 5 minutes.

2. Ladle about ¼ cup (50 mL) of the sausage mixture into prepared dish. Arrange half of the polenta slices evenly over the sausage. Spoon half of the remaining sauce and half of the mozzarella over polenta. Repeat. Sprinkle Parmesan cheese evenly over top. Bake in preheated oven until cheese is melted and mixture is bubbling, about 15 minutes.

> **PANTRY OILS**
>
> Although most vegetable oils can do double duty as salad dressings and oil for cooking, to produce the tastiest and most nutritious salads and achieve optimum cooking results, you'll need at least two different oils. The best oils for sautéing meats and vegetables, which is done over relatively high heat, are those with a high smoke point. These include peanut, canola, corn and safflower oil. Olive oil has a relatively low smoke point, which makes it unsuitable for frying, but it is high in flavor, which makes it ideal for dressing salads. The best olive oil is cold-pressed extra virgin. In addition to its superb taste, it is rich in such healthful components as essential fatty acids and vitamins A and E.

Sausage and Red Pepper Risotto

Although this recipe has a fairly long cooking time, it is actually convenient as it eliminates the constant stirring usually associated with cooking risotto. Make this using mild or hot Italian sausage depending upon your preference, and add salad and crusty rolls for a satisfying family meal.

SERVES 4 TO 6

Start to finish: 50 minutes

TIPS: Be sure to use short-grain Arborio rice when making risotto as its high-starch content is essential to produce the necessary creaminess.

For best results, stir the risotto partway through cooking. This prevents the grains on top from drying out.

EASY EXTRA

✦ Top each serving with freshly grated Parmesan cheese.

✦ PREHEAT OVEN TO 350°F (180°C)
✦ OVENPROOF SAUCEPAN WITH HEATPROOF HANDLE (SEE TIP, PAGE 71)

1 tbsp	vegetable oil	15 mL
1 lb	Italian sausage, removed from casings	500 g
1 cup	diced onion	250 mL
1 tbsp	minced garlic	15 mL
½ tsp	salt	2 mL
	Freshly ground black pepper	
1½ cups	Arborio rice (see Tips, left)	375 mL
3 cups	chicken stock	750 mL
½ cup	white wine or water	125 mL
2	roasted red peppers, chopped	2

1. In an ovenproof saucepan, heat oil over medium heat. Add sausage and cook, breaking up with a wooden spoon, until lightly browned and no longer pink inside, about 5 minutes. Using a slotted spoon, transfer to a bowl and keep warm. Drain off all but 1 tbsp (15 mL) fat.

2. Add onion to pan and cook, stirring, until softened, about 3 minutes. Add garlic, salt, and black pepper to taste. Cook, stirring, for 1 minute. Add rice and cook, stirring, until all the grains are coated with oil.

3. Add stock and wine. Bring to a boil. Stir in roasted red peppers and reserved sausage meat. Bake in preheated oven, stirring partway through cooking, until rice has absorbed liquid, about 30 minutes.

East-West Chili Pork

This tasty pork stir-fry combines that perennial North American favorite, tomato ketchup, with prepared Asian sauces. Serve over hot white rice, accompanied by a steamed green vegetable for a fast and delicious meal.

SERVES 4

Start to finish: 15 minutes

EASY EXTRA

✦ Garnish with finely chopped green onion.

1 tbsp	vegetable oil	15 mL
1 lb	pork tenderloin, cut into ½-inch (1 cm) thick slices	500 g
	Freshly ground black pepper	
¼ cup	soy sauce	50 mL
¼ cup	ketchup	50 mL
¼ cup	water	50 mL
2 tbsp	packed brown sugar	25 mL
1 tsp	Asian chili sauce	5 mL
	Hot white rice	

1. In a skillet, heat oil over medium heat. Add pork and cook, turning once, until just a hint of pink remains in the center, about 4 minutes. Season liberally with black pepper. Transfer to a warm platter.

2. Add soy sauce, ketchup and water to pan and cook, stirring, until mixture comes to a boil and thickens, about 1 minute. Stir in brown sugar and Asian chili sauce. Pour over pork. Serve over hot white rice.

ASIAN CHILI SAUCE

Don't confuse Asian chili sauce or paste, as it may be called, with tomato-based chili sauce, which is often substituted for ketchup. The Asian version, which is available in Asian markets and many supermarkets, is made from ground chilies and is very spicy. Although a great way to instantly add heat and flavor to a dish, as with all prepared foods, the quality varies from brand to brand. Try a few and find one that suits your taste.

Savory Lamb Chops

*Tasty, elegant, simple
and quick to make, this
recipe is a keeper. Serve
with mashed potatoes
and steamed green beans.*

SERVES 4

Start to finish: 15 minutes

EASY EXTRA

✦ Add 1 tsp (5 mL)
dried Italian seasoning
to oil and vinegar
dressing before
brushing lamb chops.

✦ PREHEAT BROILER OR GRILL

2 tbsp	bottled oil and vinegar dressing or Vinaigrette (see recipe, page 58)	25 mL
1 tbsp	Dijon mustard	15 mL
1½ lbs	lamb chops, thawed if frozen	750 g
2 tbsp	prepared sun-dried tomato pesto	25 mL

1. In a bowl, combine oil and vinegar dressing and mustard.

2. Pat lamb chops dry. Brush both sides with mixture.

3. Place on broiling pan about 6 inches (15 cm) from heat. Cook, turning once, until desired degree of doneness, 8 to 10 minutes. Serve topped with a dollop of pesto.

PESTO SAUCE

Pesto simply means a sauce that is pounded in a mortar, but the name has become identified with Genoese pesto, which is made from a combination of basil, garlic, pine nuts, Parmesan cheese and olive oil. The popularity of this versatile and tasty sauce has encouraged manufacturers to introduce a prepared version of it and other varieties, such as red pepper and sun-dried tomato pesto. Although these sauces are traditionally served with pasta or fish, they are an excellent way of adding flavor to a broad range of dishes.

Just Peachy Pork

Peach and pepper relish is one of my favorite condiments, and I've tried to capture its essence in this sweet and tangy sauce. Loaded with peaches it is a great accompaniment for pork. Serve over hot white rice and add an assortment of steamed vegetables in season for a delightfully different meal. Although it bakes for 30 minutes, it takes almost no time to prepare.

SERVES 4		
Prep: 15 minutes		
Baking: 30 minutes		

✦ PREHEAT OVEN TO 350°F (180°C)
✦ 8-CUP (2 L) BAKING OR GRATIN DISH

1	**can (14 oz/398 mL) sliced peaches, drained, ¼ cup (50 mL) syrup reserved**	1
1 cup	**diced green bell pepper or 1½ cups (375 mL) frozen mixed bell pepper strips**	250 mL
½ cup	**barbecue sauce**	125 mL
1 tbsp	**Dijon mustard**	15 mL
1 lb	**pork tenderloin, cut into ½-inch (1 cm) thick slices**	500 g

1. In a saucepan over medium heat, combine peaches, reserved syrup, bell pepper, barbecue sauce and mustard. Bring to a boil.

2. Reduce heat to low and simmer for 3 minutes. Place pork slices in a single layer in baking dish. Pour sauce over meat.

3. Bake in preheated oven until just a hint of pink remains, about 30 minutes.

PORK TENDERLOIN

Pork tenderloin is the most tender and juicy cut of pork. It is a great boon to convenience as it cooks quickly and produces excellent results. Widely available, fresh pork tenderloin will keep for 3 days in the refrigerator. If freezing, place in a resealable freezer bag and use within 3 months. Thaw before cooking.

Pasta and Pizza

Simple and endlessly versatile, pasta and pizza have become our easy mealtime solution. Now food manufacturers are making these Italian-inspired foods even more accessible. The variety of high-quality prepared sauces and pastas, as well as ready-to-bake pizza crusts and dough, make preparing these dishes at home as speedy as calling for delivery. Even better, those you make yourself have that cherished homemade touch. With a well-stocked pantry and the recipes in this chapter, you can put the water on to boil or preheat the oven, as the case may be, and have a delicious dinner on the table in about half an hour.

Beans and Macaroni 148

Mac and Cheese with Tomatoes 149

Fettuccine with Sweet Pea Sauce 150

Uptown Fettuccine Alfredo 152

Spinach Tortellini Bake 153

Easy Bolognese Sauce 154

Spaghetti with Broccoli 156

Penne with Tuna and Peppers 157

Pizza with Red Peppers and Goat Cheese 158

Mushroom and Artichoke Pizza 160

Gnocchi with Gorgonzola Sauce 161

Savory Mushroom and Brie Tart 162

ON HAND

✓ A good selection of dried pasta and egg noodles

✓ Two kinds of good-quality tomato sauce, such as a milder marinara-type and a spicier arrabbiata

✓ Alfredo sauce

✓ Canned tomatoes

✓ A selection of frozen vegetables, such as broccoli and/or cauliflower florets, spinach and peas

✓ Canned tuna and clams

✓ Cheese

Beans and Macaroni

This hearty weeknight dinner, which takes only 15 minutes to prepare, is a particular hit with teenage boys. Feel free to double the recipe if you need a larger quantity. Leftovers reheat well.

SERVES 4

Prep: 15 minutes
Baking: 30 to 40 minutes

TIPS: To speed up baking time, use a baking dish that is long and shallow rather than one that is square and deep.

If you're cooking for meat lovers, substitute beans with pork for the beans in tomato sauce.

If you're in a hurry, here's a way to speed up the prep time. While the macaroni is cooking, bring the beans, tomato sauce, Cheddar cheese and peppers to a simmer on the stovetop or in a microwave oven. Preheat the oven to 400°F (200°C). Combine the bean mixture and the hot macaroni as directed and top with bread crumb mixture. Bake until top is browned and mixture is bubbling, about 10 minutes.

✦ PREHEAT OVEN TO 350°F (180°C)
✦ 8-CUP (2 L) BAKING DISH, GREASED

1 cup	elbow macaroni (see Tip, page 149)	250 mL
1	can (14 oz/398 mL) beans in tomato sauce	1
2 cups	tomato sauce	500 mL
1 cup	shredded Cheddar cheese	250 mL
1	roasted red pepper, chopped	1
2 tbsp	chopped pickled hot banana peppers	25 mL
1/2 cup	dry bread crumbs	125 mL
2 tbsp	melted butter	25 mL
1 tbsp	grated Parmesan cheese	15 mL

1. Cook macaroni in a pot of boiling salted water until tender to the bite, about 8 minutes. Drain.

2. In prepared baking dish, combine hot macaroni, beans, tomato sauce, Cheddar cheese, roasted pepper and banana peppers.

3. Meanwhile, in a bowl, combine bread crumbs, melted butter and Parmesan cheese. Spread mixture evenly over macaroni mixture.

4. Bake in preheated oven until top is golden and mixture is hot and bubbling, about 30 to 40 minutes.

VARIATION: Mexican-Style Beans and Macaroni:
Substitute 1 chipotle pepper in adobo sauce, finely chopped, for the hot banana peppers and a shredded Tex-Mex cheese mix for the Cheddar.

> **MAXIMIZE CONVENIENCE**
> BY USING:
> ✦ Bottled tomato sauce
> ✦ Preshredded cheese
> ✦ Bottled roasted red peppers
> ✦ Prepared bread crumbs, such as panko

Mac and Cheese with Tomatoes

Warm, creamy and delicious, macaroni and cheese is a mealtime staple and one of our favorite comfort foods. This easy-to-make version uses Cheddar cheese soup to achieve its flavorful creaminess and canned tomatoes for a slightly piquant touch. Even better, it takes only 10 minutes to prepare.

SERVES 6

Prep: 10 minutes
Baking: 25 minutes

TIP: *Cooking Pasta* Always cook pasta (dried or fresh) in an abundance of well salted rapidly boiling water until it is tender to the bite. Combine with sauce immediately after draining, while the pasta is piping hot.

✦ PREHEAT OVEN TO 350°F (180°C)
✦ 8-CUP (2 L) BAKING DISH, LIGHTLY GREASED

12 oz	elbow macaroni (see Tip, left)	375 g
1/2 cup	dry bread crumbs	125 mL
2 tbsp	melted butter	25 mL
1	can (28 oz/796 mL) tomatoes, coarsely chopped, including juice	1
1	can (10 oz/284 mL) condensed Cheddar cheese soup	1
2 cups	shredded Cheddar cheese	500 mL
1 tsp	salt	5 mL
	Freshly ground black pepper	

1. Cook macaroni in a pot of boiling salted water until tender to the bite, about 8 minutes. Drain.

2. In a bowl, combine bread crumbs and melted butter. Set aside.

3. In a large bowl, combine tomatoes, Cheddar cheese soup, Cheddar cheese, salt, and black pepper to taste. Add hot macaroni and stir well.

4. Transfer mixture to prepared baking dish. Spread bread crumb mixture evenly over top. Bake in preheated oven until crumbs are golden and mixture is bubbling, about 25 minutes.

VARIATION: Mac and Cheese with Cauliflower: Add 3 cups (750 mL) cauliflower florets to macaroni cooking water after it has been boiling for 2 minutes. (Break up larger florets to ensure size uniformity.) Return to a boil and cook until both cauliflower and macaroni are firm to the bite, about 5 minutes. Add 1 tbsp (15 mL) basil pesto to the tomato mixture before stirring in the cauliflower mixture.

Fettuccine with Sweet Pea Sauce

I love this combination of creamy Alfredo sauce and sweet green peas.

SERVES 4

Start to finish: 20 minutes

EASY EXTRA

✦ Add 1 tsp (5 mL) grated lemon zest along with the juice.

12 oz	fettuccine (see Tip, page 149)	375 g
1 tbsp	vegetable oil	15 mL
½ cup	diced onion	125 mL
2 tsp	minced garlic	10 mL
2 cups	cooked green peas	500 mL
1 tbsp	lemon juice	15 mL
1 to 1½ cups	prepared Alfredo sauce	250 to 375 mL

1. Cook fettuccine in a pot of boiling salted water until tender to the bite, about 3 minutes if using fresh, about 5 minutes if dried. Drain.

2. In a skillet, heat oil over medium heat. Add onion and cook, stirring, until softened, about 3 minutes. Add garlic and cook, stirring, for 1 minute. Remove from heat. Stir in peas, lemon juice and Alfredo sauce.

3. In a warm serving bowl, toss fettuccine with Alfredo mixture.

VARIATIONS: Fettuccine Florentine: Substitute 1 package (10 oz/300 g) fresh spinach, stems removed and coarsely chopped, or 1 package (10 oz/300 g) frozen spinach, thawed, for the peas. Add to the skillet after garlic has been cooked. If using fresh spinach, add in batches, if necessary, and cook until wilted. (If using thawed frozen spinach, add it with liquid and cook for 5 minutes.) Remove from heat. Sprinkle with lemon juice and stir. Add Alfredo sauce and continue as directed.

Spaghetti Carbonara: Substitute 12 oz (375 g) spaghetti for the fettuccine and 4 oz (125 g) chopped pancetta or bacon for the peas. Sauté pancetta in the heated oil until it begins to brown or the bacon until it is almost crispy and transfer with a slotted spoon to a paper towel-lined plate to drain. Drain off any excess fat before softening onions and continuing with Step 2. Return cooked meat to pan along with Alfredo sauce.

Uptown Fettuccine Alfredo

Alfredo sauce is traditionally served with fettuccine because the broad flat noodles grasp the thick creamy sauce, but it works well with ridged pastas, too. Some prepared Alfredo sauces are a bit heavy, but a little freshly grated lemon zest adds a welcome tang as well as flavor.

SERVES 4

Start to finish: 15 minutes

TIP: Use other kinds of pasta, such as spinach-filled ravioli or tortellini in this recipe.

EASY EXTRAS

✦ Add 4 canned artichoke hearts, drained and quartered, to the Alfredo sauce, along with the prosciutto. Do not use marinated artichokes.

✦ Add 1 whole dried red chili pepper or 1 tsp (5 mL) hot pepper flakes to the pasta cooking water for a hint of spice.

12 oz	fettuccine (see Tip, page 149)	375 g
1 cup	prepared Alfredo sauce	250 mL
	Grated zest of 1 lemon	
2 oz	thinly sliced prosciutto, chopped	60 g
	Freshly ground black pepper	

1. Cook fettuccine in a pot of boiling salted water until tender to the bite, about 3 minutes if using fresh pasta, about 7 minutes if dried. Drain.

2. In a small saucepan over low heat, heat Alfredo sauce and lemon zest until warm to the touch, about 2 minutes. Transfer to a serving bowl.

3. Add prosciutto and hot pasta. Toss to coat pasta. Season with black pepper to taste. Serve.

ALFREDO SAUCE

Alfredo sauce was invented by Rome restaurateur Alfredo di Lello for Hollywood superstars Mary Pickford and Douglas Fairbanks. This rich, creamy sauce is traditionally made with butter, Parmesan cheese and heavy cream and mixed at the table, which gives it a freshness that can be difficult to recreate in a jar. Although there are very good prepared Alfredo sauces on the market, I've come across some that miss the mark. You may need to try a couple until you find one that suits your taste.

Spinach Tortellini Bake

Although most pasta is traditionally served as a first course in Italy, baked pasta has always been a main course, likely because it is usually more complicated to make and assemble than pasta tossed with a sauce. Today, convenience-oriented ingredients such as preshredded cheese and prepared stuffed pastas such as manicotti, ravioli and tortellini make it easy to serve these decadent combinations as weekday meals rather than reserving them for special occasions.

SERVES 4

Prep: 20 minutes
Baking: 20 minutes

EASY EXTRA

✦ Sprinkle with 2 tbsp (25 mL) toasted pine nuts before serving.

✦ PREHEAT OVEN TO 400°F (200°C)
✦ BAKING DISH, GREASED

1	package (16 oz/500 g) cheese-filled tortellini	1
2½ cups	tomato sauce (approx.)	625 mL
2 cups	baby spinach, washed and dried, or ½ bag (10 oz/284 mL) washed baby spinach	500 mL
2 cups	shredded mozzarella cheese	500 mL
2 tbsp	grated Parmesan cheese	25 mL

1. Cook tortellini according to package directions. Drain.

2. Spread about ½ cup (125 mL) of the tomato sauce over bottom of prepared baking dish. Top with half each of the hot tortellini and spinach. Sprinkle with half of the mozzarella and half of the remaining sauce. Repeat layers.

3. Sprinkle with Parmesan. Bake in preheated oven until cheese is melted and mixture is hot and bubbling, about 20 minutes.

CHEESES FOR PASTA AND PIZZA

There are a number of already shredded cheeses on the market, which speed up the preparation time when making pasta and pizza. Shredded mozzarella and Italian 4-cheese mix are excellent for blending into baked pastas or for spreading over pizzas. Because it is universally available, I usually recommend grated Parmesan as a finishing cheese. However, cheeses such as Asiago, which is nuttier and more flavorful than Parmesan, or Pecorino Romano, which is much sharper, may appeal to your taste. The quantities may vary depending upon how finely the cheese is grated, so taste and adjust to suit your preference.

Easy Bolognese Sauce

Gone are the days when making bolognese sauce was a time-consuming affair. This delicious sauce, which depends upon good prepared tomato sauce to jump-start the cooking process, is ready as soon as the pasta is cooked. Serve with salad for a great weeknight meal.

1 tbsp	vegetable oil	15 mL
1 lb	lean ground beef	500 g
1 cup	diced onion	250 mL
1 tbsp	minced garlic	15 mL
	Freshly ground black pepper	
2 cups	tomato sauce	500 mL
	Hot cooked pasta	

MAKES ABOUT 4 CUPS (1 L)

Start to finish: 20 minutes

EASY EXTRAS

✦ For a richer result, add 1 cup (250 mL) dry red wine after the garlic and black pepper have cooked for a minute. Bring to a boil and cook until slightly reduced, 3 to 4 minutes. Proceed with Step 3.

✦ Add ¼ cup (50 mL) whipping (35%) cream after simmering tomato sauce. Cook until heated through.

✦ Garnish each serving with finely chopped parsley to taste.

1. In a skillet, heat oil over medium-high heat. Add beef and onion. Brown, breaking up meat, until beef is no longer pink inside, about 5 minutes. Drain off all but 1 tbsp (15 mL) fat. Return pan to element.

2. Reduce heat to medium. Add garlic, and black pepper to taste. Cook, stirring, for 1 minute.

3. Stir in tomato sauce. Reduce heat to low and simmer for 10 minutes. Serve over pasta.

VARIATIONS: Sausage Bolognese: Use 1 lb (500 g) hot or sweet Italian sausage, removed from casings, instead of the beef.

Clam Bolognese: Heat oil, omit beef, and cook onion until softened, about 3 minutes. Proceed to Step 2. Add ¼ tsp (1 mL) hot pepper flakes along with the garlic. If adding wine, use white wine instead of red. Stir in 2 cans (each 5 oz/142 g) baby clams, drained and rinsed, along with the tomato sauce.

BOTTLED TOMATO SAUCE

Over the past two decades, the proliferation of a wide range of premium pasta sauces has been a great boon to convenience cooking. You can easily add variety to prepared tomato sauces by combining them with other foods or use them to jump-start the creation of more complex dishes. Because the time-consuming chopping and simmering have already been completed, when you open the jar, you are well on the way to creating meals that taste as if they have been made from scratch.

Spaghetti with Broccoli

Spaghetti topped with this simple broccoli and tomato sauce is an ideal dish to serve to vegetarians. The variations, which use canned tuna or pancetta — an Italian cured bacon available at specialty food stores or well-stocked supermarkets — are equally tasty. Serve with a tossed green salad and open a bottle of Chianti for a festive Italian-style meal.

SERVES 4

Start to finish: 20 minutes

EASY EXTRAS

+ If you prefer a more pungent sauce, add 3 to 4 finely chopped anchovies along with the garlic.
+ For additional spice, add ¼ tsp (1 mL) hot pepper flakes along with the garlic.
+ Garnish with finely chopped parsley.

12 oz	spaghetti (see Tip, page 149)	375 g
1 tbsp	olive oil	15 mL
1 cup	diced onion	250 mL
1 tbsp	minced garlic	15 mL
1 tsp	salt	5 mL
	Freshly ground black pepper	
1	can (28 oz/796 mL) tomatoes, coarsely chopped, including juice	1
4 cups	broccoli florets, thawed if frozen	1 L
	Grated Parmesan cheese	

1. Cook spaghetti in a pot of boiling salted water until tender to the bite, about 7 minutes. Drain.

2. Meanwhile, in a skillet, heat oil over medium heat. Add onion and cook, stirring, until softened, about 3 minutes. Add garlic, salt, and black pepper to taste. Cook, stirring, for 1 minute.

3. Stir in tomatoes with juice and broccoli and bring to a boil. Reduce heat to low and simmer until broccoli is tender, about 15 minutes.

4. In a warm serving bowl, toss cooked spaghetti with sauce. Pass the Parmesan.

VARIATIONS: Spaghetti with Tuna: Omit the broccoli. After the sauce has finished simmering, stir in 1 can (6 oz/160 g) flaked tuna, drained. Serve immediately.

Spaghetti with Pancetta and Hot Pepper: Add 2 oz (60 g) diced pancetta and 1 whole hot dried chili pepper along with the onion. Cook, stirring, until the pancetta is lightly browned, about 4 minutes. Continue with recipe and remove chili before serving.

MAXIMIZE CONVENIENCE
BY USING:

+ Frozen diced onion
+ Bottled or frozen minced garlic
+ Frozen broccoli florets
+ Already grated cheese

Penne with Tuna and Peppers

Here's a speedier version of a Marcella Hazan recipe that has been a household staple for years. Canned tuna has long been a great convenience food and the substitution of bottled roasted red peppers for freshly roasted dramatically reduces the preparation time.

SERVES 4

Start to finish: 15 minutes

12 oz	penne (see Tip, page 149)	375 g
4 tbsp	olive oil, preferably extra virgin, divided, plus additional for drizzling	60 mL
1 tbsp	minced garlic	15 mL
2	roasted red peppers, cut into strips	2
2 tbsp	finely chopped parsley	25 mL
2 tbsp	drained capers	25 mL
1	can (6 oz/170 g) tuna, preferably Italian, packed in olive oil, drained	1
	Freshly ground black pepper	
¼ cup	toasted croutons or 2 tbsp (25 mL) coarse dry bread crumbs	50 mL

1. Cook penne in a pot of boiling salted water until tender to the bite, about 8 minutes. Drain.

2. In a warm serving bowl, combine hot penne with 2 tbsp (25 mL) of the olive oil. Keep warm.

3. Meanwhile, in a small saucepan over low heat, heat remaining olive oil. Add garlic and cook, stirring occasionally, until light golden, about 3 minutes. Add red pepper strips and stir until well coated with oil.

4. Add parsley and capers. Stir well and remove from heat. Stir in tuna and black pepper to taste. Spread sauce attractively over top of warm penne. Sprinkle with croutons. Drizzle with olive oil and serve.

DRIED PASTA

Dried pasta, which originated in the seventh century, is certainly one of our earliest convenience foods. It comes in a wide variety of shapes and sizes designed to complement various sauces, from wispy-thin angel hair to thick ribbed tubes such as rigatoni. In general terms, smoother pastas work best with thinner oil-based sauces, while more robust varieties with curves and grooves are designed to capture thicker, chunky sauces.

Pizza with Red Peppers and Goat Cheese

Although there are times when nothing else will do, the days when pizza meant pepperoni and mushrooms are long past. Here's a delicious pizza with sophisticated ingredients that couldn't be easier.

SERVES 4 TO 6

Prep: 10 minutes
Baking 10 to 15 minutes

TIP: When using prepared pizza dough, read the package instructions and adjust this method accordingly. I like to make a thin crust and bake the dough with nothing on it for about 7 minutes. Then I brush the warm crust with the olive oil and pesto and proceed as directed, reducing the remaining cooking time to 8 to 10 minutes. Watch carefully to ensure the edges of the crust don't burn.

EASY EXTRAS

✦ Sprinkle with sliced black olives and/or sliced red onion before baking.

✦ PREHEAT OVEN TO 400°F (200°C)
✦ BAKING SHEET, LIGHTLY GREASED

1	**10-inch (25 cm) pizza crust or prepared pizza dough (see Tip, left)**	1
1 tbsp	**olive oil**	15 mL
¼ cup	**prepared sun-dried tomato pesto**	50 mL
1½ cups	**finely shredded mozzarella cheese**	375 mL
4 oz	**prosciutto or thinly sliced smoked ham**	125 g
2	**roasted red peppers, chopped**	2
4 oz	**soft goat cheese, crumbled**	125 g

1. Place crust on prepared baking sheet. Brush with oil and pesto.

2. Sprinkle mozzarella evenly over top. Tear prosciutto into thin strips and arrange evenly over cheese. Sprinkle red pepper then goat cheese evenly over prosciutto.

3. Bake in preheated oven until crust is golden and cheese is melted, 10 to 15 minutes.

VARIATION: Mini Pita Pizzas: If you don't have a pizza crust, try making mini pizzas with this recipe, using 4 to 6 pita breads. Follow the method above, leaving a ½-inch (1cm) border around the edge of the pita and reduce the cooking time to about 6 minutes, just until the cheese melts.

MAXIMIZE CONVENIENCE
BY USING:
✦ Prepared pesto sauce
✦ Bottled roasted peppers
✦ Already pitted black olives

Mushroom and Artichoke Pizza

Here's a traditional pizza made with mozzarella that remains a perennial favorite.

SERVES 4 TO 6

Prep: 15 minutes
Baking: 10 to 15 minutes

TIP: If using prepared pizza dough, read the package instructions and adjust this method accordingly. I like to make a thin crust, then bake the dough with nothing on it for about 7 minutes. Then I proceed with Step 2.

✦ PREHEAT OVEN TO 400°F (200°C)
✦ BAKING SHEET, LIGHTLY GREASED

1 tbsp	vegetable oil	15 mL
8 oz	sliced mushrooms	250 g
1 tbsp	minced garlic	15 mL
1 cup	thinly sliced red onion	250 mL
1 tbsp	lemon juice	15 mL
1/4 tsp	salt	1 mL
	Freshly ground black pepper	
1	10-inch (25 cm) pizza crust or prepared pizza dough (see Tip, left)	1
1	can (7 1/2 oz/213 mL) pizza sauce or 1 cup (250 mL) tomato sauce	1
1 cup	quartered drained canned artichoke hearts	250 mL
2 oz	thinly sliced ham, torn into bite-size pieces	60 g
10	pitted black olives	10
1 cup	shredded mozzarella cheese	250 mL
2 tbsp	grated Parmesan cheese	25 mL

1. In a skillet, heat oil over medium-high heat. Add mushrooms and garlic and cook, stirring, until mushrooms begin to brown and lose their liquid, about 7 minutes. Add onion and cook, stirring, for 1 minute. Remove from heat. Add lemon juice, salt, and black pepper to taste and stir. Set aside.

2. Place crust on prepared baking sheet. Spoon pizza sauce evenly over crust and spread mushroom mixture evenly over sauce. Arrange artichoke hearts, ham and olives over mushroom mixture. Sprinkle mozzarella evenly over top and Parmesan evenly over mozzarella.

3. Bake in preheated oven until crust is golden and cheese is melted, 10 to 15 minutes.

Gnocchi with Gorgonzola Sauce

Here's a dish for dairy lovers: pungent Gorgonzola melted in rich cream, finished with spinach and served over tiny potato dumplings. It's very rich, so I suggest serving small portions and accompanying with an abundance of a complementary vegetable, such as puréed squash.

SERVES 8 AS A FIRST COURSE OR 6 AS A MAIN COURSE

Start to finish: 15 minutes

EASY EXTRA

✦ Sprinkle with toasted pine nuts to taste just before serving.

1 lb	prepared potato gnocchi	500 g
6 oz	Gorgonzola	175 g
½ cup	whipping (35%) cream	125 mL
½	bag (10 oz/300 g) washed baby spinach (about 2 cups/500 mL)	½

1. Cook potato gnocchi according to package directions. Drain.

2. In a saucepan over low heat, combine Gorgonzola and whipping cream. Heat, stirring, until cheese is melted and mixture is smooth, about 4 minutes.

3. Stir in spinach and cook until wilted, about 1 minute. Toss with hot gnocchi and serve.

Savory Mushroom and Brie Tart

This combination of flavorful mushrooms, tomatoes, light crispy pastry and oozing hot Brie is sublime. It is best enjoyed with a knife and fork, but if you prefer a crispier crust, brush the thawed pastry with beaten egg and dust with grated Parmesan (see Tips, below).

SERVES 4 TO 6

Prep: 20 minutes
Baking: 10 to 15 minutes

TIPS: Frozen puff pastry is usually available in the freezer sections of food stores. However, package sizes are not uniform. The brand I usually use is sold in a 12-oz (375 g) package containing 2 sheets. That means you will need about 6 oz (175 g) puff pastry for this recipe.

For a crispier crust, brush the uncooked pastry with a beaten egg and sprinkle with 1 tbsp (15 mL) finely grated Parmesan cheese. Bake in preheated oven for 8 minutes, until pastry is puffed and lightly browned. Puncture with a fork and continue as directed, reducing baking time to about 10 minutes.

✦ PREHEAT OVEN TO 400°F (200°C)
✦ BAKING SHEET

1	sheet frozen puff pastry, thawed (see Tip, left)	1
1 tbsp	vegetable oil	15 mL
8 oz	sliced mushrooms	250 g
1/4 tsp	salt	1 mL
	Freshly ground black pepper	
1 tbsp	lemon juice	15 mL
2 tbsp	prepared basil pesto	25 mL
12	cherry or grape tomatoes, halved	12
6 oz	Brie cheese, with rind, thinly sliced	175 g

1. On a lightly floured board, roll pastry into a 12-by 9-inch (30 by 23 cm) rectangle. Fold edges over to form a 1/2-inch (1 cm) border. Carefully transfer to baking sheet.

2. In a skillet, heat oil over medium heat. Add mushrooms and cook, stirring, until they begin to brown and to lose their liquid, about 7 minutes. Season with salt, and black pepper to taste. Stir in lemon juice. Remove skillet from heat and set aside.

3. Spread pesto evenly over pastry, leaving a 1/2-inch (1 cm) border. Spread mushrooms evenly over top. Arrange tomato halves evenly over mushrooms. Lay cheese slices evenly over top. Bake in preheated oven until cheese is melted and crust is browned, 10 to 15 minutes.

MAXIMIZE CONVENIENCE
BY USING:
✦ Presliced mushrooms
✦ Bottled or frozen lemon juice
✦ Prepared pesto sauce

Desserts

Pity desserts. As the final course, they can easily seem like an afterthought and are often overlooked, particularly when the priority is getting dinner on the table in a hurry. But for many people, these delectable treats are the highlight of any meal, which is why it makes sense to have a few convenient sweets in your recipe repertoire. Using the recipes in this chapter, you can delight guests and family members with delicious desserts that are surprisingly quick to prepare and meet a wide range of needs, from basic to extraordinary.

Raspberry Peach Tart with Rich Lemon Crust..... 166

Blueberry Peach Toffee Crisp 167

Apple Cranberry Pandowdy..................... 168

Blueberry Buckle 170

Ginger Strawberry Fool......................... 171

Cherry Clafouti................................ 172

Pineapple Gratin 174

Down-Home Sweet Potato Pudding 175

Mandarin Orange Trifle 176

Mocha Tiramisu................................ 178

Glazed Pears with Sweet Creamy Cheese 179

Bittersweet Hot Fudge Sauce................... 180

Butterscotch Baked Peaches 180

Cranberry Pear Gingersnap Betty 182

Cherries Jubilee 183

Peaches with Raspberry Coulis
and Passion Fruit Sorbet 184

ON HAND

- ✓ Frozen raspberries, blueberries and strawberries
- ✓ Pitted cherries in syrup
- ✓ Canned peaches and pears
- ✓ Eggs
- ✓ Milk
- ✓ Butter
- ✓ Lemon cake mix
- ✓ Whipping (35%) cream or dessert topping mix
- ✓ Confectioner's (icing) sugar
- ✓ Brown sugar
- ✓ Granulated sugar
- ✓ Vanilla extract
- ✓ Almond extract
- ✓ Vanilla sugar
- ✓ Ground cinnamon
- ✓ Vanilla ice cream
- ✓ Bittersweet chocolate

◄ Raspberry Peach Tart with Rich Lemon Crust

Raspberry Peach Tart with Rich Lemon Crust

No one will believe how quick and easy it is to make this mouth-watering tart. It's delicious on its own, but if you're so inclined, add a scoop of vanilla ice cream.

SERVES 6 TO 8

Prep: 10 minutes
Baking: 20 minutes

✦ PREHEAT OVEN TO 350°F (180°C)
✦ 9-INCH (23 CM) PIE PLATE, GREASED

CRUST

1	package (18.25 oz/515 g) lemon cake mix	1
⅓ cup	butter, melted	75 mL
1	egg, beaten	1

TOPPING

1	package (10 oz/300 g) frozen raspberries, thawed, or 1½ cups (375 mL) raspberries	1
1	can (14 oz/398 mL) sliced peaches, drained, or 2 cups (500 mL) sliced peaches, thawed if frozen	1
2 tbsp	lemon juice	25 mL
2 tbsp	granulated sugar	25 mL
	Confectioner's (icing) sugar	

1. *Crust:* In a bowl, combine cake mix, butter and egg. Mix until moist dough forms. Press over bottom and up side of prepared pie plate. Bake in preheated oven until golden, about 10 minutes.

2. *Topping:* In a bowl, combine thawed raspberries, peaches, lemon juice and sugar. Spread evenly over warm cake. Return to oven and bake until fruit is warm and fragrant, about 10 minutes. Let cool for 5 minutes on a wire rack. Using a fine sieve, dust confectioner's sugar evenly over top. Serve warm.

VARIATION: Blueberry Peach Tart with Rich Lemon Crust: Substitute 1 package (10 oz/300 g) frozen blueberries, thawed, or 1½ cups (375 mL) blueberries for the raspberries in this recipe.

Blueberry Peach Toffee Crisp

Not only are peaches and blueberries a delicious combination, they create fresh interest in Grandma's crisp, traditionally made with cherries or apples. The addition of toffee bits adds flavor and crunch to the old-fashioned topping. Serve with vanilla ice cream or a big dollop of whipped cream.

SERVES 6

Prep: 10 minutes
Baking: 20 minutes

✦ PREHEAT OVEN TO 400°F (200°C)
✦ 6-CUP (1.5 L) BAKING DISH, GREASED

1	can (14 oz/398 mL) sliced peaches, drained, or 2 cups (500 mL) sliced peaches, thawed if frozen	1
1	package (10 oz/300 g) frozen blueberries, thawed, or 1½ cups (375 mL) blueberries	1
½ cup	quick-cooking oats	125 mL
½ cup	packed brown sugar	125 mL
½ cup	toffee bits	125 mL
2 tbsp	cold butter, cut into bits	25 mL
½ tsp	ground cinnamon	2 mL

1. Arrange peaches and blueberries evenly over bottom of prepared dish.

2. In a bowl, combine oats, brown sugar, toffee bits, butter and cinnamon. Using two forks or your fingers, combine until crumbly. Spread over fruit.

3. Bake in preheated oven until top is browned and fruit is bubbling, about 20 minutes.

VARIATION: Raspberry Peach Toffee Crisp: Substitute raspberries for the blueberries.

Apple Cranberry Pandowdy

A pandowdy is a deep-dish dessert usually made with sliced apples and topped with a crisp biscuit batter. Here's an easy version that uses prepared applesauce and refrigerated dough and is so good people always want seconds.

SERVES 8

Prep: 10 minutes
Baking: 25 minutes

TIPS: Both sweetened and unsweetened applesauce work equally well in this recipe. Your choice is simply a matter of taste.

If you don't have vanilla sugar, use the same quantity of granulated sugar instead or make your own (see page 174).

✦ PREHEAT OVEN TO 350°F (180°C)
✦ 6-CUP (1.5 L) BAKING DISH

2	jars (each 28 oz/796 mL) applesauce	2
½ cup	dried cranberries	125 mL
1	can (8 oz/235 g) refrigerated crescent roll dough	1
½ tsp	ground cinnamon	2 mL
1	package (1 tbsp/15 mL) vanilla sugar (see Tips, left)	1

1. In baking dish, combine applesauce and cranberries.

2. Unroll dough and separate into triangles. Cut each in half. Arrange over applesauce mixture, fitting together as closely as possible. Sprinkle with cinnamon, then vanilla sugar.

3. Bake in preheated oven until top is golden and crisp, about 25 minutes. Serve immediately.

VARIATION: Apple Raisin Pandowdy: Substitute ½ cup (125 mL) raisins for the cranberries.

Blueberry Buckle

A buckle is a member of the same family as the cobbler, betty and crisp. Basically, all are fruit baked in a sweetened topping. But instead of using crumbs or a biscuit-type dough, a buckle is made from cake batter, which is finished with a sugar topping. Serve with whipped cream or vanilla ice cream and expect requests for seconds.

SERVES 8

Prep: 10 minutes
Baking: 40 minutes

TIP: This quantity is half of a standard (18.25 oz/515 g) box of cake mix. Save the remainder in a resealable bag for another buckle.

EASY EXTRAS

✦ For a crunchy texture, add ¼ cup (50 mL) finely chopped pecans to the topping mixture.

✦ If, like me, you enjoy the flavor of lemon, add 1 tsp (5 mL) grated lemon zest to the cake batter.

✦ PREHEAT OVEN TO 375°F (190°C)
✦ 8-INCH (2 L) SQUARE BAKING PAN, GREASED

TOPPING

½ cup	packed brown sugar	125 mL
⅓ cup	all-purpose flour	75 mL
1 tsp	ground cinnamon	5 mL
3 tbsp	cold butter, cut into bits	45 mL

CAKE

2 cups	white, yellow or lemon cake mix (see Tip, left)	375 mL
2	eggs, beaten	2
½ cup	milk	125 mL
1	package (10 oz/300 g) frozen blueberries or 1½ cups (375 mL) blueberries	1
	Freshly whipped cream or vanilla ice cream	

1. *Topping:* In a bowl, combine brown sugar, flour and cinnamon. Mix to blend. Using two forks or your fingers, cut in butter until crumbly. Set aside.

2. *Cake:* In a bowl, combine cake mix, eggs and milk. Beat with a wooden spoon just until blended. Fold in blueberries. Pour mixture into prepared pan and level with a spatula. Spread topping evenly over cake.

3. Bake in preheated oven until a tester inserted in the center comes out clean, about 40 minutes.

Ginger Strawberry Fool

I first heard of fruit fools many years ago when I went to England to interview the late Elizabeth David, the great food writer. Elizabeth was so taken with these desserts that she published a booklet, "Syllabubs and Fruit Fools," for sale in her shop, and I treasure the copy she gave me then. I think of her every time I make one of these delicious treats, and I hope she would approve of this version, which suggests the addition of candied ginger.

SERVES 4

Start to finish: 10 minutes
Chilling: 1 hour

TIP: You can also use stem ginger in syrup, available in many specialty stores. Use the same quantity of ginger and substitute 2 tbsp (25 mL) of the syrup for the frozen orange juice concentrate.

EASY EXTRA

✦ Garnish with a sprig of fresh mint, if available.

✦ 4 PARFAIT OR WINE GLASSES

1	package (10 oz/300 g) frozen strawberries, thawed, or 1½ cups (375 mL) strawberries	1
2 tbsp	finely chopped candied ginger (see Tip, left)	25 mL
2 tbsp	frozen orange juice concentrate or orange-flavored liqueur, such as Cointreau	25 mL
1 cup	whipping (35%) cream	250 mL
¼ cup	confectioner's (icing) sugar	50 mL

1. In a food processor, combine strawberries, ginger and orange juice concentrate. Process just until mixture is the consistency of well-mashed fruit. (It should not be smooth.)

2. In a bowl, using an electric mixer, beat cream with sugar until soft peaks form. Gently fold in strawberry mixture. Spoon into parfait glasses and refrigerate until well chilled, about 1 hour.

VARIATION: Strawberry Orange Fool: Substitute 1 tsp (5 mL) grated orange zest or 2 tbsp (25 mL) chopped candied orange peel for the ginger.

Cherry Clafouti

Clafouti is basically a fruit pancake that is often served as a dessert in French bistros. Eaten warm it is comforting and delicious.

SERVES 4

Prep: 10 minutes
Baking: 25 minutes

TIP: I use a 9-inch (23 cm) square baking or gratin dish (about 2 inches/5 cm deep), which works perfectly for this recipe. If your baking dish is smaller, increase the baking time accordingly.

✦ PREHEAT OVEN TO 375°F (190°C)
✦ 6-CUP (1.5 L) BAKING OR GRATIN DISH (ABOUT 2 INCHES/5 CM DEEP) OR A SMALL GLASS PIE PLATE, GREASED

1	can (14 oz/398 mL) pitted cherries in syrup, drained (about 1⅓ cups/325 mL)	1
2	eggs	2
½ cup	milk	125 mL
¼ cup	granulated sugar	50 mL
3 tbsp	all-purpose flour	45 mL
2 tbsp	butter, melted	25 mL
1 tsp	grated lemon zest	5 mL
1 tsp	almond extract	5 mL
Pinch	salt	Pinch
	Confectioner's (icing) sugar	

1. Spread cherries over bottom of prepared dish.

2. In a blender or food processor, combine eggs, milk, sugar, flour, butter, lemon zest, almond extract and salt. Blend until mixture is smooth, about 1 minute. Pour over cherries.

3. Bake in preheated oven until puffed and golden, about 25 minutes. Serve warm. Dust with confectioner's sugar just before serving.

VARIATIONS: Brandied Cherry Clafouti: Use brandied cherries instead of cherries in syrup. Use 2 tbsp (25 mL) of the brandy in the batter and reduce the quantity of milk by an equal amount.

Blueberry Clafouti: Substitute an equal quantity of blueberries for the cherries.

Pineapple Gratin

Here's a tasty dessert that is particularly speedy to prepare. Mascarpone, a sweet and creamy Italian cheese, is a good accompaniment for fruit and is widely available.

SERVES 4

Start to finish: 10 minutes

✦ PREHEAT BROILER
✦ 4 RAMEKINS OR OTHER INDIVIDUAL SERVING-SIZE OVENPROOF DISHES

½ cup	mascarpone cheese	125 mL
2 tbsp	cream or milk	25 mL
1 tbsp	vanilla sugar (see below)	15 mL
1	can (14 oz/398 mL) pineapple tidbits, drained	1

1. In a bowl, combine mascarpone, cream and vanilla sugar. Mix until well blended. Set aside.

2. Divide pineapple equally among four ovenproof dishes. Spread cheese mixture evenly over top.

3. Place dishes about 2 inches (5 cm) from broiler and heat just until cheese starts to brown, 3 to 5 minutes. Serve immediately.

VARIATION: Berry Gratin: Use any individual berry for the pineapple. If using strawberries, halve or quarter if large. (To ensure an accurate measure, the pieces should be about the same size as the pineapple tidbits.)

VANILLA SUGAR

Vanilla sugar, which is widely available in the baking section of food stores in tablespoon (15 mL) packets, is a handy convenience food. If you prefer, it is very easy to make your own.

Vanilla Sugar: Combine a vanilla pod and granulated sugar in a jar. Seal tightly and set aside for at least 2 days. For a delicious instant dessert, sprinkle vanilla sugar over chunks of fresh pineapple purchased precut at the supermarket.

Down-Home Sweet Potato Pudding

This old-fashioned pudding is one of my favorite comfort food desserts. Although it takes a while to bake, using canned sweet potatoes dramatically reduces the preparation time for this southern classic. I like to serve this with a dollop of whipped cream.

SERVES 4

Prep: 10 minutes
Baking: 45 minutes

EASY EXTRAS

✦ If you like a hint of orange flavor, add the grated zest of 1 orange along with the spices.

✦ For a bit of crunch, sprinkle ½ cup (125 mL) chopped pecans evenly over the pudding before baking.

✦ PREHEAT OVEN TO 350°F (180°C)
✦ 6-CUP (1.5 L) BAKING DISH, GREASED

1	can (19 oz/540 mL) sliced sweet potatoes, drained	1
1	can (12 oz/385 mL) evaporated milk	1
1 cup	packed brown sugar	250 mL
3	eggs	3
2 tbsp	butter, melted	25 mL
2 tbsp	dark rum or 1 tsp (5 mL) vanilla	25 mL
½ tsp	ground nutmeg	2 mL
½ tsp	ground cinnamon	2 mL
	Whipped cream (optional)	

1. In a food processor, combine sweet potatoes, evaporated milk, brown sugar, eggs and butter and process until smooth. Add rum, nutmeg and cinnamon and pulse until blended.

2. Pour mixture into prepared dish. Bake in preheated oven until set, about 45 minutes. Spoon into bowls and top with whipped cream, if using.

Mandarin Orange Trifle

Here's a refreshing twist on an old favorite. The orange flavor is lighter than that of traditional trifle, and I like the hint of bitterness in the marmalade. If you still crave raspberry-based trifle, try the variation (below), which includes enticing cranberry and almond flavors.

SERVES 6 TO 8

Prep: 20 minutes
Chilling: 2 hours

TIPS: If using a dessert topping mix in this recipe, prepare according to package instructions and omit the sugar. If using a prepared dessert topping, omit the sugar.

To toast coconut: Spread on a baking sheet and place in a preheated 350°F (180°C) oven for 7 to 8 minutes, stirring once or twice.

If you prefer a non-alcoholic version of this dish, substitute an additional 1/4 cup (50 mL) orange marmalade for the liqueur. Combine with reserved syrup in a saucepan and heat gently, stirring, until marmalade melts and mixture is blended.

1	pound cake (approx. 10 oz/300 g), thawed if frozen	1
1/4 cup	orange-flavored liqueur	50 mL
1/4 cup	orange marmalade	50 mL
1	can (10 oz/284 mL) mandarin orange segments in syrup, drained, 3/4 cup (175 mL) syrup reserved	1
1	can (15 oz/425 g) vanilla custard or 2 cups (500 mL) vanilla custard	1
1 cup	whipping (35%) cream or 2 cups (500 mL) sweetened whipped dessert topping (see Tips, left)	250 mL
1/4 cup	confectioner's (icing) sugar	50 mL
2 tbsp	toasted shredded coconut (optional) (see Tips, left)	25 mL

1. On a work surface, cut cake in half horizontally, then cut into 1-inch (2.5 cm) cubes and transfer to a mixing bowl.

2. In a bowl, combine liqueur, orange marmalade and reserved orange syrup. Stir until blended. Pour evenly over cake pieces.

3. Place half of the soaked cake in a serving bowl. Top with half of the custard and half of the orange segments. Repeat layers once.

4. In a bowl, using an electric mixer, combine cream and confectioner's sugar. Beat on high speed until stiff. Spoon over top of layers. Sprinkle with toasted coconut, if using. Refrigerate until chilled thoroughly, about 2 hours.

VARIATION: Untraditional Raspberry Trifle: Substitute 1 package (10 oz/300 g) frozen raspberries, thawed, or 1 1/2 cups (375 mL) fresh raspberries for the mandarin orange segments. Use 3/4 cup (175 mL) cranberry raspberry juice or cranberry juice instead of the orange syrup and combine with 1/4 cup (50 mL) raspberry jam and 1/4 cup (50 mL) Amaretto liqueur. Garnish with 2 tbsp (25 mL) toasted sliced almonds (see Tip, page 62), if desired.

Mocha Tiramisu

In many ways, tiramisu is an Italian version of English trifle, using ladyfinger cookies instead of a dense white cake for a base. It is usually made with Marsala, a sweet Italian wine, but I prefer this combination of coffee and coffee-flavored liqueur. Be sure to use a good-quality vanilla custard or pudding and dry ladyfingers to soak up the coffee mixture.

SERVES 8

Prep: 10 minutes
Chilling: 2 hours

TIP: One cup (250 mL) whipping (35%) cream produces 2 cups (500 mL) whipped cream. If using packaged whipped dessert topping, check package instructions for making the necessary quantity for this recipe.

✦ 9-INCH (23 CM) SERVING BOWL
✦ FINE SIEVE

8 oz	mascarpone cheese	250 g
1	can (15 oz/425 g) vanilla custard or 2 cups (500 mL) vanilla custard	1
2 cups	whipped cream or whipped dessert topping (see Tip, left)	500 mL
1 cup	strong black coffee	250 mL
¼ cup	coffee-flavored liqueur	50 mL
24	ladyfinger cookies	24
1 tbsp	unsweetened cocoa powder	15 mL

1. In a bowl, using an electric mixer, beat mascarpone and custard until smooth. Fold in whipped cream. Set aside.

2. In a shallow bowl, combine coffee and coffee liqueur. Dip ladyfingers, one at a time, into mixture until soaked.

3. Arrange 12 ladyfingers in the bottom of serving bowl. Top with half of the mascarpone mixture. Repeat, finishing with mascarpone mixture.

4. Using a fine sieve, dust the mixture with cocoa powder. Refrigerate until chilled thoroughly, about 2 hours.

Glazed Pears with Sweet Creamy Cheese

Here's a mouth-watering family dessert that is delicious enough to serve to guests. It's also a great afternoon snack. I make this using fruit scones that I buy at a neighborhood coffee bar or with a superb cranberry focaccia made by a local bakery. But any sweet bread, preferably one containing fruit, works well.

SERVES 4

Prep: 10 minutes
Baking: 20 minutes

✦ PREHEAT OVEN 350°F (180°C)
✦ BAKING SHEET

4 oz	cream cheese, softened	125 g
2 tbsp	granulated sugar	25 mL
2 tbsp	lemon juice	25 mL
1 tsp	almond extract	5 mL
2	blueberry, cranberry or raisin scones, split, or 4 slices raisin bread	2
1	can (14 oz/398 mL) pear halves, drained, or 4 pear halves	1
4 tbsp	packed brown sugar, divided	60 mL

1. In a bowl, beat cream cheese, sugar, lemon juice and almond extract until smooth.

2. Place scones on baking sheet. Spread mixture evenly over scones. Top each with a pear half. Press 1 tbsp (15 mL) brown sugar over each half.

3. Bake in preheated oven until brown sugar is melted and pears are glazed, about 20 minutes.

VARIATION: Glazed Peaches with Sweet Creamy Cheese: Substitute peach halves for the pear.

Bittersweet Hot Fudge Sauce

If, like me, you get the occasional craving for a hot fudge sundae, here's a handy solution: always keep a bar of bittersweet chocolate in the pantry so you can make this mouth-watering sauce. Just make sure you have enough ice cream in the freezer.

1	bar (3 oz/90 g) bittersweet chocolate, broken into pieces	1
2 tbsp	Amaretto or orange-flavored liqueur or ½ tsp (2 mL) vanilla	25 mL
½ cup	whipping (35%) cream	125 mL
	Coffee or vanilla ice cream	

SERVES 4

Start to finish: 15 minutes

1. In a microwave-safe bowl, combine chocolate, Amaretto and cream. Cover tightly and microwave on High for 3 minutes.

2. Remove from oven and stir until chocolate is melted and mixture is smooth. Serve immediately over ice cream.

Butterscotch Baked Peaches

I love this combination of warm peaches in a butterscotch base, served over vanilla ice cream.

SERVES 6

Prep: 5 minutes
Baking: 20 minutes

✦ PREHEAT OVEN TO 350°F (180°C)
✦ 6-CUP (1.5 L) BAKING DISH, GREASED

2	cans (each 14 oz/398 mL) sliced peaches, drained	2
¼ cup	butter, melted	50 mL
¼ cup	packed brown sugar	50 mL
2 tbsp	dark rum or lemon juice	25 mL
½ tsp	ground cinnamon	2 mL
½ tsp	vanilla	2 mL
	Vanilla ice cream	

1. Arrange peaches evenly over bottom of prepared dish.

2. In a bowl, combine butter, brown sugar, rum, cinnamon and vanilla. Spoon over peaches.

3. Bake in preheated oven until hot and bubbling, about 20 minutes. Serve over vanilla ice cream.

VARIATION: Butterscotch Baked Bananas: Substitute 6 bananas, peeled and cut into quarters, for the peaches.

Cranberry Pear Gingersnap Betty

Here's my idea of the perfect finish to any meal: flavorful fruit baked in a sweetened crumb mixture. While our grandmothers used fresh fruit and homemade bread crumbs to make this traditional dessert, today's cook can take advantage of store-bought cookies to vary the crust and enhance the flavor of the fruit.

SERVES 4 TO 6

Prep: 10 minutes
Baking: 25 minutes

TIP: To save on cleanup, after making the gingersnap crumbs in a food processor, measure them, then return to the food processor work bowl. Add the sugar, ginger and butter to the crumbs and pulse to combine.

✦ PREHEAT OVEN TO 375°F (190°C)
✦ 8-CUP (2 L) BAKING DISH, GREASED

2 cups	fine gingersnap cookie crumbs (about 8 oz/250 g cookies)	500 mL
2 tbsp	granulated sugar	25 mL
1 tsp	ground ginger	5 mL
1/4 cup	butter, melted	50 mL
2	cans (each 14 oz/398 mL) pear halves, drained, 1/2 cup (125 mL) syrup reserved	2
1/2 cup	dried cranberries	125 mL
1 tbsp	lemon juice	15 mL

1. In a bowl or food processor (see Tip, left), combine cookie crumbs, sugar and ginger. Add butter and mix well.

2. Spread one-third of the crumb mixture in bottom of prepared dish. Lay half of the pears over the crumbs and sprinkle with cranberries. Spoon 2 tbsp (25 mL) of the reserved pear syrup over fruit. Repeat layers. Top with remaining crumbs.

3. Mix together remaining pear syrup and lemon juice and pour over top. Bake in preheated oven until top is golden and mixture is bubbling, about 25 minutes.

VARIATIONS: Cherry Pear Gingersnap Betty: Substitute 1/2 cup (125 mL) dried cherries for the cranberries.

Cranberry Pear Brown Betty: Substitute 2 cups (500 mL) fine bread crumbs for the gingersnap crumbs and 1 tsp (5 mL) ground cinnamon for the ginger. Add 2 tbsp (25 mL) granulated sugar to the mixture.

Cherries Jubilee

This is one of the first "gourmet" desserts I learned to make more than 30 years ago. It is still a great way of turning canned fruit into a celebratory dish. All you need is a small bottle of Kirsch, a cherry-flavored liqueur. It keeps indefinitely after opening and is useful for flavoring many fruit desserts.

SERVES 4

Start to finish: 15 minutes

TIP: If you prefer a non-alcoholic version of this dish, substitute an additional $1/4$ cup (50 mL) red currant jelly for the Kirsch. Warm in a saucepan over low heat until it melts, then combine with lemon zest, sugar and cherries. Omit Step 5.

$1^1/_2$ cups	drained canned or bottled cherries, with 1 cup (250 mL) plus 2 tbsp (25 mL) syrup reserved	375 mL
4 tbsp	Kirsch or brandy, divided	60 mL
1 tbsp	grated lemon zest	15 mL
1 tbsp	vanilla sugar or granulated sugar	15 mL
2 tbsp	red currant jelly	25 mL
1 tbsp	cornstarch	15 mL
	Vanilla ice cream	

1. In a bowl, combine drained cherries, 2 tbsp (25 mL) of the Kirsch, lemon zest and vanilla sugar. Toss to combine and set aside.

2. In a skillet over medium heat, bring 1 cup (250 mL) of the reserved cherry syrup to boil. Reduce heat and simmer until reduced by half, about 5 minutes. Stir in red currant jelly until dissolved. Reduce heat to low.

3. Add cherry mixture and cook, stirring, until cherries are heated through, about 2 minutes.

4. In a bowl, dissolve cornstarch in remaining 2 tbsp (25 mL) cherry syrup. Add to cherry mixture and cook, stirring, until thickened, about 2 minutes. Remove from heat.

5. Sprinkle remaining Kirsch over hot cherry mixture and ignite. Bring flaming pan to the table and spoon cherry mixture over vanilla ice cream.

Peaches with Raspberry Coulis and Passion Fruit Sorbet

Don't be put off by the fancy name — a coulis is just a thick, puréed sauce and, with the help of a food processor, nothing could be easier to make. This dessert is so good — and all you do is turn on the food processor and assemble it.

SERVES 6

Start to finish: 15 minutes

TIPS: If you prefer a seedless coulis, put the mixture through a fine sieve after processing.

Use canned peach halves, drained; frozen peaches, thawed; or fresh freestone peaches, in season.

✦ 6 DESSERT DISHES

¾ cup	fresh raspberries or ½ package (10 oz/300 g) unsweetened frozen raspberries, thawed	175 mL
1/4 cup	granulated sugar	50 mL
1 tbsp	lemon juice	15 mL
6	large scoops passion fruit or lemon sorbet	6
6	peach halves (see Tips, left)	6

1. In a food processor, combine raspberries, sugar and lemon juice. Process until smooth. Refrigerate until ready to use.

2. Place 1 scoop sorbet in a dessert dish. Top with a peach half and drizzle with raspberry coulis. Serve immediately.

CANNED AND FROZEN FRUIT

Canned and frozen fruit is a good replacement for fresh, particularly during the winter when fresh fruit travels so far to reach northern markets. If processed with little or no sugar, it tastes good and the nutrients are comparable to fresh. If you're concerned about additives or pesticides, many natural foods stores have an excellent selection of processed fruit that is organically certified.

National Library of Canada Cataloguing in Publication

Finlayson, Judith
 The convenience cook: 125 best recipes for easy homemade meals using time-saving foods from boxes, bottles, cans & more / by Judith Finlayson.

Includes index.
ISBN 0-7788-0073-3

1. Cookery. 2. Cookery (Canned foods) 3. Cookery (Frozen foods) 4. Convenience foods.
I. Title.

TX714.F55 2003 641.5 C2003-901471-1

Index

A

Aïoli, about, 20
Alfredo sauce, about, 152
  Creamy Corn and Shrimp, 104
  Fettuccine Florentine, 150
  Fettuccine with Sweet Pea Sauce, 150
  Paupiettes of Sole Florentine, 99
  Seafood on Toast, 32
  Spaghetti Carbonara, 150
  Uptown Fettuccine Alfredo, 152
Almonds, toasting, 62
  Chicken Salad Amandine, 62
Anchovies, about, 22
  Anchovy Spread, 22
  Chicken Provençal, 108
  Tapenade, 22
  Tapenade-Stuffed Eggs, 22
Anchovy paste, about, 29
  Cheesy Anchovy Toasts, 29
Appetizers
  Asparagus with Tunnato, 17
  Basil and White Bean Spread, 25
  Cheesy Anchovy Toasts, 29
  Crab Louis, 20
  Crostini, 29
  Egg and Chive Spread, 24
  Egg and Olive Spread, 24
  Egg and Roasted Red Pepper Spread, 24
  Ham and Red Pepper Dip, 66
  Hummus with Tahini, 21
  Mexican Pita Pizzas, 26
  Refried Nachos, 26
  Roasted Red Pepper Dip, 16
  Seafood on Toast, 32
  Shrimp-Stuffed Avocado, 18
  Smoked Oyster Hummus, 21
  Smoked Salmon and Red Caviar Mousse, 28
  Tapenade, 22
  Tapenade-Stuffed Eggs, 22
  Tunnato Spread, 17
  Tunnato-Stuffed Eggs, 17
Apple Cranberry Pandowdy, 168
Apple Raisin Pandowdy, 168
Artichokes
  Chicken and Artichoke Bake, 112
  Mushroom and Artichoke Pizza, 160
Asian chili sauce, 142
Asian Cucumber Salad, 63
Asparagus with Tunnato, 17
Avocados, about, 18
  Avocado Salad, 76
  Beet and Avocado Salad, 64
  Palm Hearts Niçoise, 67
  Shrimp-Stuffed Avocado, 18

B

Bacon
  New England Clam Chowder, 51
  Spaghetti Carbonara, 150
Baked Fish with Tomatoes and Roasted Red Pepper, 98
Bananas
  Butterscotch Baked Bananas, 180
Basil pesto sauce, about, 143
  Squash and White Bean Soup with Basil Pesto, 38
  Scrambled Eggs with Pesto, 75
Beans, about, 25, see also Kidney and Black beans
  Basil and White Bean Spread, 25
  Beans and Macaroni, 148
  Beans, Beef and Biscuits, 136
  Beef and Biscuits, 136
  Mexican-Style Beans and Macaroni, 148
  Simple Succotash, 77
Beans, refried
  Chicken Tacos, 118
  Enchiladas in Salsa Verde, 80
  Refried Nachos, 26
Beef, ground
  Beans, Beef and Biscuits, 136
  Chili con Carne Pronto, 130
  Crispy Shepherd's Pie, 126
  Easy Bolognese Sauce, 154
  Salisbury Steak with Mushroom Gravy, 127
Beef, roast
  Thai-Style Beef Salad, 54
Beef, sirloin
  Beef and Broccoli with Rice Stick Noodles, 131
  Beef Stroganoff, 134
  Chinese Pepper Steak, 128
  Steak Creole, 132
Beets, about, 64
  Beet and Avocado Salad, 64
  Beet and Celery Salad, 64
  Beet and Feta Salad, 64
  Borscht, 46
  Red Flannel Hash, 135
Berry Gratin, 174
Biscuits, about, 21
Bittersweet Hot Fudge Sauce, 180
Black beans
  Chicken and Black Bean Chili, 116
  Chicken, Sausage and Black Bean Chili, 116
  Eggs Rancheros with Black Bean Sauce, 76
  Sausage and Black Bean Chili, 138
  Squash and Black Bean Chili, 86
  Zesty Black Bean Pie, 78
Blueberries
  Blueberry Buckle, 170
  Blueberry Clafouti, 172
  Blueberry Peach Tart with Rich Lemon, 166
  Blueberry Peach Toffee Crisp, 167
Borscht, 46
Brandied Cherry Clafouti, 172
Bread crumbs, about, 113
Breads, about, 21
Broccoli
  Beef and Broccoli with Rice Stick Noodles, 131
  Broccoli and Cheddar Cheese Soup, 40
  Spaghetti with Broccoli, 156
Bruschetta with Beans, 59
Butterscotch Baked Bananas, 180
Butterscotch Baked Peaches, 180

C

Carrots
  Orange and Onion Salad, 56
  Carrot, Orange and Onion Salad, 56
  Chili Cheddar Soup, 42
Cauliflower
  Cauliflower Gratin, 82
  Creamy Cauliflower Soup with Smoked Salmon, 44
  Creamy Cauliflower Soup, 44
  Mac and Cheese with Cauliflower, 149
  Mulligatawny Soup, 44
Celery, about, 136
  Beet and Celery Salad, 64
Celery seed, about, 130
Cheese, about, 153, see also Cream cheese and Feta
  Beans and Macaroni, 148
  Berry Gratin, 174
  Best-Ever Baked Chicken, 113
  Broccoli and Cheddar Cheese Soup, 40
  Cauliflower Gratin, 82
  Cheese and Hash Brown Omelet, 74
  Cheesy Anchovy Toasts, 29
  Chicken Tacos, 118
  Chili Cheddar Soup, 42
  Eggs Rancheros with Black Bean Sauce, 76

Enchiladas in Salsa Verde, 80
Gnocchi with Gorgonzola
  Sauce, 161
Great Grilled Cheese
  Sandwich, 33
Lentil Shepherd's Pie, 81
Mac and Cheese with
  Cauliflower, 149
Mac and Cheese with
  Tomatoes, 149
Mexican-Style Beans and
  Macaroni, 148
Mocha Tiramisu, 178
Mushroom and Artichoke
  Pizza, 160
Pineapple Gratin, 174
Pizza with Red Peppers and Goat
  Cheese, 158
Refried Nachos, 26
Sausage Polenta Lasagna, 139
Savory Mushroom and Brie
  Tart, 162
Spinach Tortellini Bake, 153
Sumptuous Chicken Sandwich
  with Brie, 30
Tomato Gratin, 82
Tomato Rarebit, 33
Cherries
  Brandied Cherry Clafouti, 172
  Cherries Jubilee, 183
  Cherry Clafouti, 172
  Cherry Pear Gingersnap
    Betty, 182
Chicken, breasts, about, 116
  Best-Ever Baked Chicken, 113
  Chicken and Black Bean
    Chili, 116
  Chicken Provençal, 108
  Chicken, Sausage and Black Bean
    Chili, 116
  Chicken Tacos, 118
  Chinese Chicken, 110
  Sausage and Black Bean Chili, 116
  Spicy Peanut Chicken, 117
Chicken, cooked
  Chicken and Artichoke Bake, 112
  Chicken Curry, 109
  Chicken Salad Amandine, 62
  Chicken Salad Sandwich, 62
  Mulligatawny Soup, 44
  Orange and Onion Chicken, 114
  Sumptuous Chicken Sandwich
    with Brie, 30
Chicken, cutlets
  Italian-Style Chicken Cutlets, 120
  Turkey Cutlets in Savory
    Cranberry Gravy (variation), 122
Chicken, ground
  Turkey Sloppy Joes, 121
Chicken, rotisserie, about, 114
  Orange and Onion Chicken, 114
  Chicken Curry, 109
  Chicken Provençal, 108

Chicken, thighs
  Chinese Chicken, 110
Chickpeas
  Falafel in Pita, 84
  Smoked Oyster Hummus, 21
  Warm Chickpea Salad, 58
Chilies
  Chicken and Black Bean
    Chili, 116
  Chicken, Sausage and Black Bean
    Chili, 116
  Chili Cheddar Soup, 42
  Chili con Carne Pronto, 130
  Very Veggie Chili, 86
Chinese Chicken, 110
Chinese Pepper Steak, 128
Chocolate
  Bittersweet Hot Fudge Sauce, 180
Clams
  Clam Bolognese, 154
  New England Clam Chowder, 51
Classic Cream of Tomato Soup, 50
Cocoa powder
  Mocha Tiramisu, 178
Coconut milk
  Coconut Shrimp Curry, 103
  Thai-Style Salmon Curry, 90
Corn
  Chicken Tacos, 118
  Corn Chowder, 39
  Creamy Corn and Shrimp, 104
  Ginger Chili Sweet Potato
    Soup, 43
  Mexican-Style Scrambled Eggs, 75
  Simple Succotash, 77
  Squash and Black Bean Chili, 86
  Very Veggie Chili, 86
Corned beef
  Red Flannel Hash, 135
Crab
  Crab Foo Yung with Chinese
    Vegetables, 70
  Crab Louis, 20
  Seafood on Toast, 32
Cranberries
  Apple Cranberry Pandowdy, 168
  Cranberry Pear Brown Betty, 182
  Cranberry Pear Gingersnap
    Betty, 182
Cranberry sauce
  Turkey Cutlets in Savory
    Cranberry Gravy, 122
Cream cheese
  Anchovy Spread, 22
  Glazed Peaches with Sweet
    Creamy Cheese, 179
  Glazed Pears with Sweet Creamy
    Cheese, 179
  Salmon Quiche, 95
  Zesty Black Bean Pie, 78
Creamy Cauliflower Soup, 44
Creamy Cauliflower Soup with

Smoked Salmon, 44
Creamy Corn and Shrimp, 104
Crisps
  Blueberry Peach Toffee Crisp, 167
  Raspberry Peach Toffee Crisp, 167
Crispy Shepherd's Pie, 126
Crostini, 29
Crudités, about 17
Cucumbers, about, 63
  Asian Cucumber Salad, 63
  Cucumbers in Sour Cream, 63
Cumin seeds, toasting, 76
Curried Lentil and Spinach Soup, 47
Curries
  Chicken Curry, 109
  Coconut Shrimp Curry, 103
  Thai-Style Salmon Curry, 90

D
Desserts
  Apple Cranberry Pandowdy, 168
  Apple Raisin Pandowdy, 168
  Berry Gratin, 174
  Bittersweet Hot Fudge Sauce, 180
  Blueberry Buckle, 170
  Blueberry Clafouti, 172
  Blueberry Peach Tart with Rich
    Lemon Crust, 166
  Blueberry Peach Toffee Crisp, 167
  Brandied Cherry Clafouti, 172
  Butterscotch Baked Bananas, 180
  Butterscotch Baked Peaches, 180
  Cherries Jubilee, 183
  Cherry Clafouti, 172
  Cherry Pear Gingersnap
    Betty, 182
  Cranberry Pear Brown
    Betty, 182
  Cranberry Pear Gingersnap
    Betty, 182
  Down-Home Sweet Potato
    Pudding, 175
  Ginger Strawberry Fool, 171
  Glazed Peaches with Sweet
    Creamy Cheese, 179
  Glazed Pears with Sweet Creamy
    Cheese, 179
  Mandarin Orange Trifle, 176
  Mocha Tiramisu, 178
  Peaches with Raspberry Coulis
    and Passion Fruit Sorbet, 184
  Pineapple Gratin, 174
  Raspberry Peach Tart with Rich
    Lemon Crust, 166
  Raspberry Peach Toffee Crisp, 167
  Strawberry Orange Fool, 171
  Untraditional Raspberry
    Trifle, 176
Dips, see Appetizers
Down-Home Sweet Potato
  Pudding, 175
Dressings, see Vinaigrettes

E

East-West Chili Pork, 142
Easy Bolognese Sauce, 154
Easy Tartar Sauce, 92
Eggs, about, 74
  Best-Ever Scrambled Eggs, 75
  Cheese and Hash Brown Omelet, 74
  Crab Foo Yung with Chinese Vegetables, 70
  Egg and Black Olive Crostini, 24
  Egg and Chive Spread, 24
  Egg and Roasted Red Pepper Spread, 24
  Egg Foo Yung with Chinese Vegetables, 70
  Eggs Rancheros with Black Bean Sauce, 76
  Hard-cooked, 55
  Italian-Style Poached Eggs, 72
  Mediterranean Potato Salad, 60
  Mexican-Style Scrambled Eggs, 75
  Palm Hearts Niçoise, 67
  Poached, 72
  Savory Egg Salad Sandwich, 24
  Scandinavian Pasta Salad, 55
  Scrambled Eggs with Fine Herbs, 75
  Scrambled Eggs with Pesto, 75
  Scrambled Eggs with Smoked Salmon, 75
  Shrimp Foo Yung with Chinese Vegetables, 70
  Spinach Frittata, 71
  Tapenade-Stuffed Eggs, 22
  Tunnato-Stuffed Eggs, 17
Enchiladas in Salsa Verde, 80

F

Falafel in Pita, 84
Feta cheese
  Beet and Feta Salad, 64
  Roasted Red Pepper Dip, 16
  Shrimp in Tomato Sauce with Feta, 102
Fettuccine, see also Pasta
  Fettuccine Florentine, 150
  Fettuccine with Sweet Pea Sauce, 150
  Uptown Fettuccine Alfredo, 152
Fish, see also individual varieties and Seafood
  Baked Fish with Tomatoes and Roasted Red Pepper, 98
  Pan-Fried Halibut in Spicy Lemon Sauce, 96
  Parmesan-Crusted Snapper with Tomato Olive Sauce, 91
  Paupiettes of Sole Florentine, 99
  Potato Pancakes with Smoked Salmon, 94
  Salmon Burgers, 92
  Salmon Quiche, 95
  Thai-Style Salmon Curry, 90
Fruit, canned and frozen, about, 184

G

Garlic Chili Shrimp, 100
Garlic-Infused Olive Oil, 25
Ginger Chili Sweet Potato Soup, 43
Ginger Strawberry Fool, 171
Glazed Peaches with Sweet Creamy Cheese, 179
Glazed Pears with Sweet Creamy Cheese, 179
Gnocchi with Gorgonzola Sauce, 161
Great Grilled Cheese Sandwich, 33
Ground beef, see Beef, Ground

H

Halibut
  Baked Fish with Tomatoes and Roasted Red Pepper, 98
  Pan-Fried Halibut in Spicy Lemon Sauce, 96
Ham
  Ham and Red Pepper Dip, 66
  Mushroom and Artichoke Pizza, 160
  Savory Palm Hearts Salad, 66
  Scandinavian Pasta Salad, 55
Hearts of palm, about, 67
  Ham and Red Pepper Dip, 66
  Palm Hearts Niçoise, 67
  Savory Palm Hearts Salad, 66
Herb-Flavored Vinaigrette, 60
Hummus
  Hummus with Tahini, 21
  Smoked Oyster Hummus, 21

I

Italian-Style Chicken Cutlets, 120
Italian-Style Poached Eggs, 72

J

Just Peachy Pork, 144

K

Kidney beans
  Bruschetta with Beans, 59
  Chili con Carne Pronto, 130
  Salami and White Bean Salad, 59
  Squash and White Bean Soup with Basil Pesto, 38
  Tuscan Bean Salad, 59
  Very Veggie Chili, 86

L

Lamb chops
  Savory Lamb Chops, 143
Lemons
  Blueberry Buckle, 170
  Blueberry Peach Tart with Rich Lemon, 166
  Lemony Lentil Soup with Spinach, 47
  Raspberry Peach Tart with Rich Lemon Crust, 166
Lentils
  Curried Lentil and Spinach Soup, 47
  Lemony Lentil Soup with Spinach, 47
  Lentil Shepherd's Pie, 81
Lobster
  Seafood on Toast, 32
Louis Sauce, 20

M

Macaroni
  Beans and Macaroni, 148
  Mac and Cheese with Cauliflower, 149
  Mac and Cheese with Tomatoes, 149
  Mexican-Style Beans and Macaroni, 148
Mandarin Orange Trifle, 176
Mayonnaise, about, 17, 20
Meats, about, 12
Mediterranean Potato Salad, 60
Mexican Pita Pizzas, 26
Mexican-Style Beans and Macaroni, 148
Mexican-Style Scrambled Eggs, 75
Mini Pita Pizzas, 158
Mocha Tiramisu, 178
Mulligatawny Soup, 44
Mushrooms
  Beef Stroganoff, 134
  Mushroom and Artichoke Pizza, 160
  Salisbury Steak with Mushroom Gravy, 127
  Savory Mushroom and Brie Tart, 162

N

New England Clam Chowder, 51
Noodles, see also Pasta
  Beef and Broccoli with Rice Stick Noodles, 131
  Beef Stroganoff, 134

O

Oats
  Blueberry Peach Toffee Crisp, 167
  Raspberry Peach Toffee Crisp, 167

Oils, about, 139
Olives
    Egg and Black Olive Crostini, 24
    Egg and Olive Spread, 24
    Parmesan-Crusted Snapper with
        Tomato Olive Sauce, 91
Onions, about, 56
    Carrot, Orange and Onion
        Salad, 56
    Orange and Onion Chicken, 114
Oranges
    Carrot, Orange and Onion Salad, 56
    Ginger Strawberry Fool, 171
    Mandarin Orange Trifle, 176
    Orange and Onion Chicken, 114
    Strawberry Orange Fool, 171
Oysters
    Smoked Oyster Hummus, 21

P

Palm Hearts Niçoise, 67
Pan Bagna, 34
Pancetta
    Spaghetti Carbonara, 150
    Spaghetti with Pancetta with Hot
        Pepper, 156
Pan-Fried Halibut in Spicy Lemon
    Sauce, 96
Parmesan-Crusted Snapper with
    Tomato Olive Sauce, 91
Pasta, about, 149, 157, see also
    Noodles
    Beans and Macaroni, 148
    Clam Bolognese, 154
    Easy Bolognese Sauce, 154
    Fettuccine Florentine, 150
    Fettuccine with Sweet Pea
        Sauce, 150
    Gnocchi with Gorgonzola
        Sauce, 161
    Mac and Cheese with
        Cauliflower, 149
    Mac and Cheese with
        Tomatoes, 149
    Mexican-Style Beans and
        Macaroni, 148
    Penne with Tuna and Peppers, 157
    Sausage Bolognese, 154
    Scandinavian Pasta Salad, 55
    Spaghetti Carbonara, 150
    Spaghetti with Broccoli, 156
    Spaghetti with Pancetta with
        Hot Pepper, 156
    Spaghetti with Tuna, 156
    Spinach Tortellini Bake, 153
    Uptown Fettuccine Alfredo, 152
Paupiettes of Sole Florentine, 99
Peaches
    Blueberry Peach Tart with Rich
        Lemon, 166
    Blueberry Peach Toffee
        Crisp, 167
    Butterscotch Baked Peaches, 180

Glazed Peaches with Sweet
    Creamy Cheese, 179
Just Peachy Pork, 144
Peaches with Raspberry Coulis
    and Passion Fruit Sorbet, 184
Raspberry Peach Tart with Rich
    Lemon Crust, 166
Raspberry Peach Toffee Crisp, 167
Pears
    Cherry Pear Gingersnap Betty, 182
    Cranberry Pear Brown Betty, 182
    Cranberry Pear Gingersnap
        Betty, 182
    Glazed Pears with Sweet Creamy
        Cheese, 179
Peas
    Chicken and Artichoke Bake, 112
    Cream of Green Pea Soup, 48
    Cream of Green Pea Soup with
        Mint, 48
    Fettuccine with Sweet Pea Sauce,
        150
    Thai-Style Salmon Curry, 90
Peppers, about roasting, 16, see
    also Roasted red peppers
    Chinese Pepper Steak, 128
    Just Peachy Pork, 144
    Roasted Red Pepper Dip, 16
    Spicy Peanut Chicken, 117
    Steak Creole, 132
Pesto sauce, about, 143, see also
    Basil pesto
Pineapple Gratin, 174
Pine nuts, toasting, 85
Pizza
    Mexican Pita Pizzas, 26
    Mini Pita Pizzas, 158
    Mushroom and Artichoke
        Pizza, 160
    Pizza with Red Peppers and Goat
        Cheese, 158
    Savory Mushroom and Brie
        Tart, 162
Poached eggs, 72
Pork, tenderloin, about, 144
    East-West Chili Pork, 142
    Just Peachy Pork, 144
Potatoes, about 42, see also Sweet
    Potatoes
    Cheese and Hash Brown Omelet,
        74
    Chili Cheddar Soup, 42
    Corn Chowder, 39
    Creamy Cauliflower Soup, 44
    Crispy Shepherd's Pie, 126
    Enchiladas in Salsa Verde, 80
    Lentil Shepherd's Pie, 81
    Mediterranean Potato Salad, 60
    New England Clam Chowder, 51
    Potato Pancakes with Smoked
        Salmon, 94
    Red Flannel Hash, 135
    Tomato Gratin, 82

Poultry, see Chicken and Turkey
Prosciutto
    Pizza with Red Peppers and Goat
        Cheese, 158
    Uptown Fettuccine Alfredo, 152

R

Raspberries
    Peaches with Raspberry Coulis
        and Passion Fruit Sorbet, 184
    Raspberry Peach Tart with Rich
        Lemon Crust, 166
    Raspberry Peach Toffee Crisp, 167
    Untraditional Raspberry Trifle, 176
Red Flannel Hash, 135
Red pepper, see Roasted red pepper
Refried Nachos, 26
Rice, cooking, 110
    Sausage and Red Pepper Risotto,
        140
    Spinach Risotto, 85
Roast beef, Thai-Style Beef Salad, 54
Roasted red peppers, 16
    Baked Fish with Tomatoes and
        Roasted Red Pepper, 98
    Egg and Roasted Red Pepper
        Spread, 24
    Ginger Chili Sweet Potato Soup,
        43
    Ham and Red Pepper Dip, 66
    Penne with Tuna and Peppers, 157
    Pizza with Red Peppers and Goat
        Cheese, 158
    Roasted Red Pepper Dip, 16
    Sausage and Red Pepper
        Risotto, 140
    Smoked Oyster Hummus, 21
Rotisserie chicken, about, 114
    Chicken Curry, 109
    Chicken Provençal, 108
    Orange and Onion Chicken, 114

S

Salad dressings, see Vinaigrettes
Salads, about salad greens, 11
    Asian Cucumber Salad, 63
    Asparagus with Tunnato, 17
    Avocado Salad, 76
    Beet and Avocado Salad, 64
    Beet and Celery Salad, 64
    Beet and Feta Salad, 64
    Carrot, Orange and Onion Salad, 56
    Chicken Salad Amandine, 62
    Cucumbers in Sour Cream, 63
    Mediterranean Potato Salad, 60
    Palm Hearts Niçoise, 67
    Salami and White Bean Salad, 59
    Savory Palm Hearts Salad, 66
    Scandinavian Pasta Salad, 55
    Thai-Style Beef Salad, 54
    Tuscan Bean Salad, 59
    Warm Chickpea Salad, 58